THE GOSPEL DAY BY DAY
THROUGH LENT

$2.50

The Gospel day by day through Lent

BRIAN MOORE SJ

A Liturgical Press Book

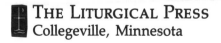
THE LITURGICAL PRESS
Collegeville, Minnesota

Cover by Fred Petters

Copyright © 1988 by Brian Moore. All rights reserved. First published in 1988 by St. Paul Publications, Homebush, New South Wales, Australia. This edition for the United States of America and Canada published by The Liturgical Press, Collegeville, Minnesota.

Printed in the United States of America.

2	3	4	5	6	7	8	9

Library of Congress Cataloging-in-Publication Data
Moore, Brian A.
    The Gospel day by day through Lent / Brian Moore.
        p.   cm.
    ISBN 0-8146-2002-7
    1. Lent—Prayer-books and devotions—English.   2. Bible N.T.
Gospels—Meditations.   I. Title
BX2170.L4M67   1992
242'.34—dc20   91-40716
                                                              CIP

Contents

Foreword

The purpose of this book is to provide help to people who wish to reflect on the daily gospel readings set down for the Season of Lent and to make some application of them to their own day to day lives. These reflections, it is hoped, may also prove useful in the preparation of homilies.

In length, the reflections on the weekday readings run to about four hundred words while those for the generally more leisured Sundays are twice that length.

On the first two Sundays of Lent the gospel readings, whatever the year, narrate the same incidents — the Temptation and the Transfiguration of Christ, taken in turn from each of the synoptics. It seemed sufficient, therefore, to give only one reflection for those Sundays, as also for Passion (Palm) Sunday. In the case of the other Sundays where the gospel reading differs from year to year reflections are given on each of the readings of the three year cycle.

Introduction
The Meaning of Lent

When Pope St Leo the Great (+ 461) referred to Lent as, 'These forty days instituted by the Apostles', he was stretching things a bit. Doubtless, the necessity of prayer, fasting and alms-giving figured in the Apostles' preaching — as it had in the preaching of the Prophets, of John the Baptist and of Jesus himself; but the history of the evolution of the forty days of Lent as a liturgical Season is quite a lengthy one.

In the earliest centuries, the duration of Lent varied from place to place; here, one day; there, two days; elsewhere, forty hours. And the severity of the fast has fluctuated wildly — as it has even in the last hundred years. It was not until the end of the 4th century that a duration of forty days became universal. In the West, since every Sunday was reckoned a little Easter, there were in fact only thirty-six penitential days. To bring the days of actual penance up to forty, the western Church in the 7th century added four extra days, beginning with Ash Wednesday.

This fixing on the number forty has plenty of biblical pre-cedents. For example, Moses was on the mountain for forty days; Israel wandered in the wilderness for forty years; Elijah walked for forty days to come to Horeb, the mountain of God — to name but a few of many. In the New Testament we read of Jesus' fasting in the wilderness for forty days; and the days between the Lord's Ascension and the day of Pentecost are numbered forty.

However, it is not the duration of these days or years which is of significance; the important thing is what was consequent on them. After forty days Moses was given the Ten Commandments; on arrival at Horeb, Elijah had a deep personal experience of God. After forty days of prayer and fasting, Jesus entered into combat with the Adversary; after 'persevering in prayer' for forty days, the infant Church was anointed with the Holy Spirit.

These forty days or years were simply preliminaries — necessary, rigorous periods of preparation for some climactic event. This is important to an understanding of the nature of Lent. Just as none of those periods of days or years in either Testament was an end in itself, so neither is Lent nor the most scrupulous observance of Lent an end in itself.

Lent is intelligible only in the light of its climax, Easter. The beginning is in ashes; the end is the paschal fire. The discipline of Lent is not an end in itself but a time of preparation of oneself to enter as fully as possible, in mind and heart, into the Paschal Mystery of the death and resurrection of Jesus — and of our own in union with him.

This is, perhaps, why the Liturgy of Lent refers to the period as 'this joyful Season'. The joy has its source not here and now but is anticipatory — as the anticipated thrill of the actual contest might infuse an athlete's training for it.

For this reason, too, while the Liturgy constantly places before us the necessity of a change of heart, of prayer, fasting ('Which means,' says St Leo, 'not simply a reduction of food but the elimination of our evil habits') and almsgiving ('which, under the general name of mercy — St Leo again — 'covers a multitude of praiseworthy deeds of charity') it also constantly turns our attention to Baptism. For our Baptism is our first definitive sacramental entering into the Paschal Mystery.

Hence, Vatican 2 says:
The lenten Season has a two-fold character: 1) it recalls Baptism or prepares for it; 2) it stresses a penitential spirit. By these means especially, Lent readies the faithful for celebrating the

Paschal Mystery after a period of closer attention to the Word of God and more ardent prayer. In the Liturgy itself and in Liturgy-centered instructions, these baptismal and penitential themes should be more pronounced.

With just such an emphasis on a penitential theme Lent begins — the reception of the ashes on Ash Wednesday.

In the Old Testament, sprinkling oneself with ashes or sitting in them or, even, eating them was symbolic of an acute awareness of one's own mortality, the transitoriness of life, of mourning, and of repentance. Such, too, is their liturgical significance, as is evident from the alternative formulas employed as the ashes are imposed:

Repent, and believe in the Good News.
Remember, man, that you are dust and into dust you will return.

But we bow our heads to receive these cold grey ashes at the beginning of Lent only with a view to warming ourselves at the bright Easter fire at its end.

First Four Days of Lent

Ash Wednesday
Matthew 6:1-6, 16-18

In today's reading, Jesus commends the 'good deeds' of the religious tradition in which he himself was brought up and which his Church has inherited — almsgiving, prayer and fasting. These things, as do all religious observances, constantly run the risk of formalism and, worse, of having their very purpose perverted through egotism, so that all becomes ostentation and the seeking of 'men's admiration'.

To counter this, Jesus urges secrecy. But this, too, has its own temptation to personal self-satisfaction, to smugness in the knowledge that one is doing good. To conceal one's doing good from others is very often easily done; it is more difficult to conceal it from oneself, not letting our left hand know what our right hand is doing.

An excessive fear of falling into one or other of these two traps would, of course, lead to a kind of paralysis, and Jesus elsewhere commands that our light shine in the sight of men so that, seeing our good works, they might give praise to our heavenly Father. Here, therefore, he urges us to consider only one audience, one witness to our actions — our Father who sees all. The more we direct our attention to him the less will we take notice of our own or of others' reactions to what we do.

To live in the presence of God, to constantly call him to mind in raising our hearts to him, is the surest way to that singleness of purpose, that purity of intention which Jesus is here telling us has to be the motive of all our works. Our judgment on our observance of Lent, then, is to be based not on how little we have eaten or how much we have given away, but on the deepening of our awareness of God's presence to us and his action in our lives. 'In him we live and move and have our being'; while he dwells in us, giving us being, growth, sensation, and causing us to know him, and making us his temple since we are created in his image and likeness.

The whole of Lent is a summons to a change of heart, and the depth of that change of heart will be commensurate with the deepening of our awareness of God and of ourselves in relationship to him.

There are, says St John Chrysostom, 'five high roads to a change of heart: first, acknowledging one's sins; second, forgiving the sins of others; third, prayer; fourth, almsgiving; fifth, humility' — all which comprise the special endeavour of this joyful Season.

Thursday After Ash Wednesday
Luke 9:22-25

By linking Jesus' prophecy of his impending passion (the first of several in Luke) with his laying down as a condition of following him the necessity of taking up one's cross daily, Luke makes several points: that, in Augustine's words, 'The trials of this life are the passion of Christ in us' — not merely bad things which befall us or are inflicted on us; that Jesus is the Way we must follow, and that this following of him involves sharing his sufferings; that this carrying of the cross is a day to day affair, a life-long imperative; that, as in the case of Jesus himself, our striving must be to transcend a patient acceptance of the cross in our lives and come to a willing embracing of it, for in the cross is our salvation and by it we are set free — first from the bondage of sin and finally from the bonds of death itself.

Such a following of Jesus requires that we 'deny ourselves'. Such self-denial is something more than those things we call acts of self-denial. It is a radical renunciation of self and of self-will, a going out of ourselves that God might enter, an emptying of ourselves in order to be so filled with the spirit of Jesus that we might say with St Paul, 'For me, to live is Christ', and, 'I live now not I but Christ lives in me'. It is for this purpose — 'that we might live no longer for ourselves but for him who died and rose for us' — that the Holy Spirit has been given us, without whose help such a renunciation of self and an embracing of the cross in the spirit in which Jesus embraced his, are impossible.

This is the importance of those exterior acts of self-denial, that bodily asceticism to which we attend more particularly during Lent: they remind us of, and help us to achieve interior self-denial, that spiritual asceticism through which we offer our whole selves as a spiritual sacrifice acceptable to God.

Paradoxically, as Jesus here assures us, it is by renouncing ourselves that we truly find ourselves; it is by dying to self and to all self love that we come to live, and to live in freedom. For, by doing these things we come to have in us the mind that was in Christ Jesus, come to have one will and one heart with him who alone is the Truth and the Life.

Friday After Ash Wednesday
Matthew 9:14-15

In the Gospel reading for Ash Wednesday we heard Jesus say, 'When you fast . . .'. Clearly, he takes it for granted that his followers will continue the three practices of the Jewish religious tradition — almsgiving, prayer, fasting. In today's reading, therefore, Jesus is certainly not saying that fasting is unnecessary or irrelevant. He is, in fact, not directly answering the question which John's disciples put to him. He is, instead, drawing their attention to himself and who he is.

The coming of the Messiah and his Kingdom was, in the tradition of the questioners, pictured under the imagery of a banquet; and it was their belief that religious practices such as fasting would hasten his coming. Jesus, therefore, points to the fact that his disciples do not fast as a sign that the Messiah has come and that the Kingdom has been inaugurated.

However, Jesus' bodily presence on earth is only temporary and the Kingdom only incohate. There will come a time, therefore, when fasting will be an appropriate religious exercise — until the time of his second, definitive, coming and the consummation, in perfection, of the Kingdom.

Jesus' reference to himself as the bridegroom means that the banquet which represents the Kingdom is a wedding feast and that, just as the Old Testament sometimes represented Israel as the bride of God, so the new Israel, the Kingdom, the Church is the bride of Christ. The union between Christ and his Church is everything that, ideally, a marriage is — betokening union, mutual love, mutual fidelity, and the giving of life.

What Christ is to the Church he is, also, to the individual. He desires that he and each of his followers should be united in love in a faithful and life-giving oneness of heart and mind. It is to achieving and deepening this union that a follower of Christ directs his life, taking Jesus as the supreme love of his life in which all other loves exist; and it is inasmuch as they greatly promote this union that the traditional practices of prayer, almsgiving and fasting have their meaning and value. Thus prayer expresses the desire of Christ's follower to have a relationship with him which is truly a comm-union; almsgiving is the recognition of his presence in others; and fasting expresses a hunger which he alone can satisfy.

Saturday After Ash Wednesday
Luke 5:27-32

The alacrity with which Levi accepts the call of Jesus to follow him gives us, perhaps, cause for shame at the thought of how resistant we are to doing the same; and the fact that he expresses his joy at that call in so extravagant a manner also, perhaps, gives us cause for shame at the thought of how half-heartedly, even grudgingly, we respond to his saying, 'Come' — resigning ourselves to, rather than willingly embracing the cross to which that call might summon us.

Jesus, by accepting Levi's invitation to a banquet at which all the guests, save he, are sinners, enables those sinners to accept his invitation to that banquet which is eternal life in the Kingdom of God. But the conditions of obtaining an invitation to that banquet is that they who are invited must acknowledge that they are sick and in need of a physician, that they are sinners in need of a saviour. And one of the aims of this season of Lent is to help us sincerely to make this acknowledgment — that we are sick and in need of healing, sinful and in need of the saving grace of Christ.

In this incident, the Pharisees and their scribes are not present as invited guests, for their self-righteousness (ironically termed 'virtuousness' by Jesus) excludes them; but they are among the guests as critics, fault-finders. As Jesus says of them elsewhere, they will not make their way into the Kingdom themselves but hinder from entering those who would.

When these critics demand of the disciples, 'Why do you eat with tax collectors and sinners?' the disciples are evidently too cowed to reply, for it is Jesus himself who answers them — in Matthew's version, using Hosea's words of long before, 'What I want is mercy, not sacrifice'. Solicitude for the exact observance of dietary laws means nothing if it is not matched with a like solicitude for the spiritual health of others and care for them. Long ago, God, through Isaiah, had confronted them: 'Is not this the sort of fast that pleases me: to break unjust fetters . . ., to let the oppressed go free . . ., to share your bread with the hungry, shelter the homeless poor, and clothe the man you see to be naked?'

Our dispositions of heart towards others and the helpful actions they inspire are the real measure of our observance of Lent; for we have a Master who not only eats and drinks with sinners but who gives them his own flesh to eat and blood to drink.

First Week of Lent

First Sunday of Lent
Year A □ Matthew 4:1-11
Year B □ Mark 1:12-15
Year C □ Luke 4:1-13

The Gospel reading for the first Sunday of Lent is always a narrative of the temptation of Jesus in the wilderness. Mark tells the story in two verses:

> Immediately afterwards (i.e. after his baptism by John) the Spirit drove him out into the wilderness and he remained there for forty days and was tempted by Satan. He was with the wild beasts and the angels looked after him.

Mark seems to imply that the whole period was one of testing — only the fact of which, not its nature, he records. Matthew and Luke put the time of testing at the end of the forty days — and the days of fasting, not mentioned by Mark — and describe, in varying order, three instances of testing of Jesus by the Tempter. Matthew introduces the ministering angels only after Satan has been routed (Mark has them present all the time) while Luke does not mention them at all.

Instead, Luke ends his account quite ominously: 'Having exhausted all these ways of tempting him, the Devil left him — to return at the appointed time'. The 'appointed time' is that of the Passion, in which Jesus confronts sin and death and definitively conquers them. This, presumably, is why Luke prefers to locate the last of the three wilderness temptations in Jerusalem, the scene of Jesus' passion and resurrection.

The mysteries of the life of Jesus are inexhaustible; it is not surprising, therefore, that each of the Evangelists would contemplate this incident from different, yet converging, points of view. Mark's saying, 'He was with the wild beasts' (they are not presented as threatening or a danger, but as a simple fact) recalls Adam in his state of primal innocence. Perhaps then, for Mark, Jesus is the new Adam, the new embodiment of the human race who will not, as Adam did, fail in the time of

23

testing. Matthew clearly, from Jesus' quotations from the Book of Deuteronomy, sees Jesus as the embodiment of a faithful Israel which had proved itself unfaithful in the time of its testing throughout forty years in the wilderness. Luke seems to concentrate more directly on Jesus as Son of God and on what this sonship meant.

The three tests to which Jesus is put — to change stones into loaves, to inaugurate his ministry with a dazzling display, to accept the kingdoms of the world at the hands of an other than his father — all revolve around Jesus' mission as Son. Presumably this is why they are recorded — to prevent any false understanding of the nature of Jesus' sonship and mission, and to teach us that trust in God (an unconditional and not would-be manipulative trust) is the essence of both sonship and service of God.

Jesus manifests his unique sonship of God by being supremely God's servant. No, he will not use his miraculous powers to his own advantage. No, he will not blackmail his Father into seeing that no harm befalls him. No, he will not receive kingship over the whole of creation except at the hands of the One who said to him, 'Ask, and I will give you the nations for your heritage, the ends of the earth for your domain' (Ps 2). Nor will he win that kingship in any other way than that willed by his Father — that is, through the cross; and, nailed to it, he will no more accept the challenge, 'If you are the Son of God, come down from the cross' than he will accept the present challenge, 'If you are the Son of God, cast yourself down from here'.

Similarly, throughout his public ministry, Jesus refuses to give the kind of 'sign' asked for by 'a wicked generation'.

For our encouragement, St Augustine makes a rather wonderful point:

In his own body he prefigures us who are members of that body. When he willed to be tempted by the Devil, he figuratively transferred us into himself. In Christ, you were being tempted, because Christ had his human flesh from you (i.e. had the same human nature as we have). He suffered the temptation for you;

and of himself won the victory for you. If we have been tempted in him, in him we conquer the Devil. Recognize your own self — tempted in him, and also conquering in him. He might have avoided the Devil completely; but, had he not been tempted, he would have failed to give you the lesson of conquering when you are tempted.

Essentially, any trials or temptations which we undergo are testings of our sonship of God, of our willingness to trust him absolutely as we conscientiously try to discover and follow his will for us. The thing which Moses urged the people of Israel to learn from their forty years in the wilderness is what we try to learn from our times of being tested: 'Learn from this that the Lord your God was training you as a man trains his child' (Deut 8:5). And it is to us as much as to his Apostles that Jesus says, 'Satan, you must know, has got his wish to sift you all like wheat' (Lk 22:31).

The thing is, we are never alone in time of testing. Jesus' being tested was done under the aegis of the Holy Spirit who 'led', even 'drove', him into the wilderness for that very purpose. So, too, we who are sons of God are led by the Spirit of God (Rom 8:14).

Again, we have not only the example of Jesus to strengthen us; we have, also, his active compassion. As the *Letter to the Hebrews* says (in 2:18 and 4:15), 'Because he himself has been through temptation, he is able to help others who are tempted'; and, 'It is not as if we had a high priest who was incapable of feeling our weaknesses with us; but we have one who has been tempted in every way that we are, though he is without sin'.

First Week
Monday
Matthew 25:31-46

The verse which immediately follows today's reading runs, 'Jesus had now finished all he wanted to say'. This reading, then, is for Matthew Jesus' farewell discourse to his disciples before his passion. It is his final word on what it means to be a follower of his, a word delivered in a vividly realised setting of majesty, judgment and finality — all indicative of its utter seriousness; and that final word is 'love'. The criterion by which all who have ever lived will be judged is active love of the neighbour.

However, this active love of the neighbour is not simply philanthropy. It is love grounded in the belief that Jesus has chosen to be identified with every individual member of the human race into which he entered by his incarnation and for each member of which he freely accepted death. This identification ensures his continuing presence among us, and that presence is most readily recognised in those who are most in need — the poor, the suffering, the victims — for they most vividly reproduce the pattern of Jesus' own life on earth. In ministering to them we minister to Jesus, who was himself the perfect servant of God. Just as his contemporaries' various attitudes towards Jesus himself revealed their varying understandings of God, so our attitude towards our fellow human beings reveals our understanding of Jesus and, therefore, also of God. Faith underpins charity and charity gives life to faith.

This identification of Jesus with individuals works in two ways; for if Jesus thus identifies himself with every individual human being he does so, also, with me. His word is, therefore, that I should act as he did. An active love for others means more than simply doing good, more than fulfilling a duty. It is our being what Jesus has made us — one with him.

What we call the Last Judgment, then, is in fact a continuous judgment on us at every moment we call 'now'. Hence, in this passage of the Gospel we find two totally different groups of people — the 'blessed' and the 'accursed' — expressing their surprise in exactly the same words: 'Lord, when did we see you ...?' The accursed do not see him because they separate Jesus from the individual with whom Jesus identifies himself. The blessed do not see him because their faith that Jesus is in everyone in need, and in themselves, and the actions which spring from this faith are not a matter of role-playing but the dynamic of their lives.

First Week
Tuesday
Matthew 6:7-15

Reconciliation, whether between man and God or man and man, is the result of repentance on the part of the offender and forgiveness on the part of the offended against. And reconciliation in both of these dimensions (man — God, man — man) is the desired fruit of the observance of Lent. Reconciliation is not a static either/or thing, achieved once and for all. It is dynamic; and, having been achieved radically, it can become deeper, more profound, as repentance grows more sincere and forgiveness matures into love.

It is evident that reconciliation between man and man cannot come about unless forgiveness responds to repentance (or, more soundly, repentance responds to already perceived forgiveness — on the model of, 'Lord, you overlook man's transgressions in order that he might repent'). Forgiveness by the offended should precede, not wait for, repentance by the offender.

In today's reading, Jesus introduces a whole new dimension: reconciliation with God can not be achieved solely on a one to one basis. Reconciliation with God first requires reconciliation with one's fellows. We can not draw near to God by distancing ourselves from our neighbour or by by-passing him, whether it is we who have offended our neighbour or the neighbour has offended us. Just as reconciliation between man and man can not be effected without a mutual repentance/ forgiveness, so an individual's reconciliation with God is dependent on that individual's reconciliation with his fellows — as a triangle can not have an apex without having a base.

God's mercy is, so to speak, an inexhaustible stream which can not flow until man has removed the obstacles which restrict it. That is why Jesus speaks so insistently and so uncompromisingly on the necessity of heart-felt forgiveness of and genuine reconciliation with others. 'If you do not forgive others' failings, your heavenly Father will not forgive yours'; 'Offering a gift at the altar? — first, be reconciled to your brother, then offer'; 'How often must you forgive a brother? — seventy times seven times'; and his parable of the servant who would not forgive his fellow servant (Mt 18:23-35) ends with the solemn warning, 'That is how my heavenly Father will treat you unless you each forgive your brother from your heart'.

There is in this teaching no room for our saying, 'He should have known better', and using that as an excuse for withholding forgiveness or not actively seeking reconciliation; for this same Jesus will say of his executioners, 'They know not what they do', and forgive them from the depths of a heart pierced with a lance.

First Week
Wednesday
Luke 11:29-32

When Jesus' contemporaries ask for a sign they are asking for some spectacular miracle which would establish his credentials as being sent by God and provide them with a motive for believing in him. Yet they had witnessed miracles enough; and, far from coming to faith in Jesus, they had attributed his powers to diabolical intervention. Signs of the kind they had in mind are powerless to move a heart that is hardened; indeed, evident miracles serve only to harden it further — as we see from their saying, 'It is through the Prince of devils that he casts out devils'. Jesus tells them that they have it all wrong.

Far from needing a sign of accreditation, he himself is the sign of salvation which God has given to mankind — just as Jonah, whose mission of preaching to the people of Nineveh was not confirmed by any such signs, was a sign of the salvation God was offering them. As Son, Jesus is so much greater than Jonah and, therefore, a surer and more universal sign. As Wisdom incarnate, he is so much greater than Solomon whose proverbial wisdom was sufficient to draw the Queen of the South to Jerusalem to hear him. If such lesser signs from God were recognised, and acted upon, by the people to whom they were given, rightly will the people of those times condemn the refusal of faith on the part of Jesus' contemporaries. Faith in Jesus and the repentance it leads to will subsequently lead the believer to the realisation that God has visited his people and brought them salvation.

The Gospels are written for believers. If, then, Luke records these words of Jesus he does so for us, for our good — for us who, in fact, do believe that Jesus is the God-given, the God-become-man sign of our salvation.

The point of today's reading for us is, then, that we who believe in Jesus should do as the people of Nineveh did who believed in Jonah's preaching — repent, make new our hearts. Repentance is not a once-off thing, an act of mind and heart performed once and for all. It is, or should be, the dynamic of our life — a continuing growth in the appreciation of who we are, and of who God is, and of what should be the relationship existing between us.

During Lent, therefore, we might profitably at different times measure ourselves against the many metaphors the Scriptures use to describe this relationship: we are his sheep, his people, his temple, his children ... but always his.

First Week
Thursday
Matthew 7:7-12

At the heart of the prayer of petition, which Jesus here urges upon us, we find a humble recognition of our utter dependence on God and a trust-filled confidence that he will hear our prayers; and this confidence itself is a recognition of the fatherly goodness of God. The prayer of petition, then, rightly made, is of great importance, since it keeps before us the right relationship between ourselves and God: we are both creature and child of God; and to emphasise either of these at the expense of the other is to introduce an imbalance into that relationship. As well, the prayer of petition is a constant exercise of the faith we have that God is good.

'Ask ... Seek ... Knock ...': Jesus uses imperatives, each of which conjures us an image of an earnest searcher — which images elsewhere expand into parables which illustrate various aspects of prayer: e.g. the importunate friend (Lk 11:5-8), the unjust judge (Lk 18:1-8), and so on. But here, all Jesus is concerned with is that we should pray, and pray with urgency, perseverence and joy.

These qualities inhere in our prayers not because of who we are who pray but because of who he is to whom we pray. We pray to a Father who is wholly good, who will not mock his children's prayers or answer them with things which are useless or harmful. Jesus recognises the 'evil' which can be found in people; he recognises that earthly fathers are capable of neglect of their children and even be lacking in love for them. Nevertheless, he chooses the image of a benevolent and provident parent as best describing the God to whom we pray — the one who alone, he says, is good, and from whom all fatherhood in heaven or on earth takes its name.

To this exhortation to prayer, Matthew adds 'the golden rule': 'Always treat others as you would like them to treat you'. In adding this, Matthew certainly reflects the mind of Jesus. When, for example, Jesus talks of God's forgiveness he invariably links it to our forgiveness of others. Here, the implication is that we can not expect to receive from God if we are unwilling to give to others.

As the prayer of petition arises out of and deepens the relationship between ourselves and God, so a willingness to ask and to be asked promotes the relationship which could exist between people who are all children of the one good Father.

First Week
Friday
Matthew 5:20-26

The theme of today's reading is reconciliation; and Lent is, above all, the season in which we especially strive to become more and more profoundly reconciled to, and one with God; and more sincerely reconciled to, and at peace with our fellow human beings. Indeed, as Jesus makes quite clear in this passage when he mentions the worship of God, our willingness to be reconciled to our fellows is not only a sign of but, in fact, a pre-requisite of our being reconciled to God. Reconciliation, we know, is not a static state achieved once and for all; it is a constant striving for a deepening harmonisation of our will with the will of God; it is a deepening of good-will towards others: and both of these are grounded in love.

'To hate your brother is to be a murderer,' writes John (1 Jn 3:15). This is what Jesus is saying here. Just as later (in v. 28) he says that lust in the heart is already adultery, so hatred in the heart is tantamount to murder. It is not merely that hatred and anger can lead to verbal or physical assault or, even, to murder. The point is, in Jesus' mind, anger and hatred are a kind of spiritual murder. By murder, a murderer wishes to eliminate another, wishes to get that other out of his life — which is exactly what hatred does: it excludes another person from one's life and consideration, annihilates that person as far as one is concerned. Yet it is God who wills that that other should live, and has made him in his own image and likeness. Anger and hatred are ultimately a proud usurping of a power God alone may wield.

Jesus is telling his hearers that they must interiorise their outward observance of the Law; and he says the same to us. The authority on which he does this is himself: 'I say to you'; and as he himself is the authority for his demands, so he himself is our model in our striving to fulfill them. The Litany names him as 'our peace and reconciliation' — for, as Paul says, 'God was in him reconciling the world to himself' (2 Cor 5:19) through his self-sacrificing death on the cross (Rom 5:10). This ministry of reconciliation (which is possible only through love and self-sacrifice) Jesus entrusts to every one of his followers when he says, 'Blessed are the peacemakers for they shall be called children of God'.

First Week
Saturday
Matthew 5:43-48

In Leviticus 11:45 we read, 'You must be holy because I (Yahweh) am holy'. However, the text goes on: 'Such is the law concerning animals, birds and all living creatures . . . to separate the clean from the unclean'. The holiness there commanded is simply an external, ritual holiness. But here, when Jesus says, 'You must be perfect as your heavenly Father is perfect', he is commanding something profoundly internal — a personal holiness of heart which will manifest itself in a love for all other fellow human beings, a love which is as universal and, so to speak, as undiscriminating as the love of God who is Love.

It is his love which manifests God's perfection. Our striving for perfection, then, is not an effort to acquire all the virtues, but to grow in that two-fold love of God and neighbour without which the virtues lose their soul, that two-fold love which encompasses in itself every virtue. 'Without love,' says St Paul, 'I am nothing'; and eloquence, prophecy, spiritual understanding, faith, almsgiving and self-sacrifice are of no avail.

This love towards others is not something based on nearness of kinship, common interests or the experience of being loved first. Loves of this kind, Jesus says, are the common property of humanity. Genuine love embraces all these, but embraces, also, enemies and persecutors. Just as the sun shines and the rain falls equally on all, so our love is imperfect as long as anyone is excluded from its ambit. Nor is love perfect if it is simply non-hatred. Love is to be active. 'If your enemy is hungry,' says St Paul, 'feed him'. Love is to be given even when it is not reciprocated; and persecutors are to be prayed for.

Persecution is, of course, a very relative thing and may range from a mere flea-bite to martyrdom. Similarly, a persecutor may be one who lacerates us, or simply irritates. And human nature may find it easier to forgive, to pray for and to love a great persecutor (because this feeds a sense of our own magnanimity) than a petty persecutor (for it is natural to feel that such a person should be beneath contempt). But forgiveness based on pride is not forgiveness at all, for it is self-regarding and not concerned for the other.

As God is love, and acts only out of love, so it is only attitudes and actions which are motivated by love which merit the promised reward — our becoming true sons of our heavenly Father, acknowledged as such by him.

Second Week of Lent

Second Sunday of Lent
Year A □ Matthew 17:1-9
Year B □ Mark 9:1-9
Year C □ Luke 9:28-36

As on the first Sunday of Lent, so also today: whatever the Cycle, the Gospel reading is always a narrative of the Transfiguration of Jesus.

All three evangelists lead up to their accounts of the Transfiguration by narrating the same three preceeding events. First, Jesus asks his disciples, 'Who do people say I am? Who do you say I am?' He then goes to foretell his passion, death and resurrection. Finally, he gives notice that anyone who would be a follower of his must renounce himself and take up his cross.

The Transfiguration of Jesus confirms Jesus' prophecy of his passion, for Moses and Elijah speak of the 'passing' which Jesus is to accomplish in Jerusalem — his 'exodus', his passage through the Red Sea of death into the Promised Land of immortal glory in his resurrection. Thereby, Peter's false notion of what was implied in his answer to Jesus' question about who he was, 'You are the Christ of God', is corrected — for Peter had responded to Jesus prophecy of his passion with, 'This must not happen to you, Lord!' To be the Christ, the Anointed One, of God meant to be anointed to sacrifice before being anointed to glory.

The Transfiguration also gives the Father's answer to the question, 'Who is this Jesus?' The 'staging', so to speak, of the Transfiguration makes it clear that Jesus is on a unique plane, even in comparison with such personages as Moses and Elijah. For Jesus is already transfigured when they appear, and they depart after the Father's voice is heard proclaiming Jesus to be his Son, the Chosen, the Beloved. And Jesus is alone when the Father gives the disciples the command, 'Listen to him'.

Moses and Elijah, that is to say the Law and the Prophets, were for a time — to give their testimony to Jesus in whom their own missions are brought to completion and the Law and the prophecies are fulfilled. Jesus remains — the one, all-sufficient Teacher to whom all must listen. So the *Letter to the Hebrews* begins:

> At various times in the past and in various different ways, God spoke to our ancestors through the Prophets; but in our own time, he has spoken to us through his Son . . .;

and Paul writes to the Romans, 'the Law has come to an end with Christ' (10:4) for, as he tells the Galatians, 'the Law was to be our guardian until Christ came' (3:23-29).

In view of the third of the preliminaries to the Transfiguration (i.e. Jesus' words to his followers about taking up their cross) it is commonly said that the reason for the Transfiguration's taking place was to strengthen, in advance, the faith of the Apostles who would witness the utter abasement of Jesus in the Agony in the Garden. For us who know Jesus to be the Word made flesh and who understand his words that 'it was necessary for the Christ to suffer and so enter into his glory', this third aspect naturally most preoccupies us in reflecting on today's reading.

Possibly, the Church always gives us this incident on this day to encourage us (who know ourselves to be beset by weakness and temptation, as we find in reflecting on the gospel of the first lenten Sunday) to take heart at the sight of the glory that shall be ours as the crowning of our perseverence.

As the embers of Ash Wednesday can be fanned into the paschal fire, so can the trials and weaknesses which afflict us for a time be regarded as so many pledges of future and eternal glory.

Last week, St Augustine pointed out that Jesus underwent trial, and conquered, in that self same human nature which is ours; and that, therefore, in him we are conquerers also. Similarly, of the Transfiguration of Jesus Pope St Leo the Great writes that in it

> the foundation of his holy Church's hope was laid — so that the whole Body of Christ should realize the nature of the change which it must undergo, and that the members might promise

themselves a share in that glory which has already shone around their Head.

And here Leo cites the Lord's saying that, at his coming, 'the righteous will shine like the sun in the Kingdom of their Father', and St Paul's saying, 'I consider that the sufferings of this present time are not worth comparing with the glory which is going to be revealed in us'.

Finally, we might draw one further helpful reminder from this scene. Peter, deciding that 'It is good for us to be here' (as we, too, are here in heart and mind through prayer) wants the experience to continue. But the experience is transitory, and looking up they see 'only Jesus', their familiar, day-to-day Jesus. We, too, have to recognise that to be a follower of Jesus means that we can not always be 'with him on the holy mountain' (2 Pet 1:18). We must also sometimes make the dark descent with him into the garden of Gethsemane and (again, with him and in his footsteps) climb the hill of Calvary.

Second Week
Monday
Luke 6:36-38

Jesus' first injunction, 'Be compassionate as your Father is compassionate', is virtually a summary of the whole of the fourteenth chapter of Luke's gospel in which we read of the shepherd's concern for a single lost sheep and a father's compassion for a returning wayward son. In those parables there is no condemnation of the silliness of the sheep or of the fatal free choice of the son. There is only concern for the lost one, and rejoicing over the home-coming. This is the universal, unquestioning compassion of our Father which Jesus bids us imitate. To be compassionate towards another's undeserved misfortunes is, perhaps, easy enough. It is not so easy when the unfortunate other has, out of personal wilfulness, embarked on a course which could only lead to grief. Jesus commands us to share, in another sense, that grief.

The chief obstacle to experiencing and expressing compassion in the case of people who have brought misfortune on themselves is that tendency which we experience to judge and, having judged, to condemn: 'You brought it on yourself; don't expect any sympathy from me'. The reaction is natural; but Jesus is insisting that we rise above it and become 'co-mourners' with the father in the parable, 'co-mourners' with Jesus who prayed, 'Father, forgive them; they know not what they do'.

'Blessed are they who mourn' — over others, over their loss and misfortunes rather than judge and condemn — 'for they shall be comforted' — in the knowledge that, refraining from judgment, they themselves will not be judged, and that, refraining from condemnation, they themselves will not be condemned.

And when we are the injured party, 'Grant pardon, and you will be pardoned'. Again a Beatitude is invoked: 'Blessed are the merciful, for they shall obtain mercy'. More than we in our being injured, the person who injures himself in injuring us is in need of compassion, and compassion begins with the granting of pardon, and pardon is to be given unconditionally — independently, even, of the contrition of the one who has injured us.

These are the things regarding which we are commanded, 'Give'. We are to give, in full measure, those things of which, in full measure, we are ourselves so much in need — the compassion and the mercy of the one heavenly Father of us all.

Second Week
Tuesday
Matthew 23:1-12

Knowing ourselves, we all know someone who is at times guilty of what Jesus here rebukes — the failure to practise what we preach, the failure to see to it that our conduct and actions are in harmony with our professed beliefs and attitudes. This is not necessarily the hypocrisy which Jesus here denounces. Even in ourselves, and still more in others, we must make allowance for those inconsistencies between word and deed which spring from simple human weakness. What Jesus denounces is a hardness of heart which, habitually, not only divorces the external from the interior but uses the external to present a picture of a non-existent interior. It is an attitude of exploiting the weaknesses or, even, the virtues of others in order to promote self-righteousness.

Thus, Jesus says, 'They tie up heavy burdens and lay them on men's shoulders'. By their interpretations of the Law and the consequent accumulation of a multiplicity of minute prescriptions, they make the observance of the Law a misery, if not an impossibility, for ordinary people. Thereby, they themselves, appear by contrast as paragons of religious observance. As such, they claim titles and places of honour; and the respect for, the devotion to the Law which the ordinary people have, leads them to accord them these outward signs of recognition. But all the while, behind the facade of dignity, lurks vanity; and the titles of 'father', 'master' and 'teacher' do not name things as they are but simply feed ambition and pride.

So, too, the phylacteries. They were little boxes containing the chief texts of the Law and were bound on arm or brow to keep the Law before their eyes; and the tassels were meant to recall the Commandments. These they made broader and longer than those of others, with the implicit claim to greater devotion to and observance of the Law. But it was all show — just as a multiplicity of devotional objects and practices is not necessarily an indication of greater devotion to, love of God.

What Jesus was asking of his contemporaries he asks of us — true religion, which is the worship of God in spirit and in truth and not in mere external observances, which are as lifeless as a body from which the spirit has departed.

This is the humility which exalts us in the judgment of God — that, as Jesus says elsewhere, our worship of God and our helping our neighbour be done 'in secret', as far as that can be. And to this admonition he adds the promise, 'and your Father who sees all that is done in secret will reward you'.

Second Week
Wednesday
Matthew 20:17-28

Three times Jesus foretold his passion and each time his own disciples, far from understanding and offering him their compassion, withdrew from him and turned in on themselves and their own concerns — which is what we do if we do not really listen to others. After the first prophecy, Peter presumes to remonstrate with Jesus. After the second, the disciples argue among themselves as to who is the greatest. After the third, we have the ambition of the sons of Zebedee, John and James, and their mother. Their ambition is based on a misunderstanding of the nature of the Kingdom in which they aspire to be important. Because of the nature of the Kingdom, it is not in Jesus' gift to grant them the positions they desire. He can give them only a share in his passion, without which entrance itself into the Kingdom cannot be gained.

Jesus is very gentle with the presumption and ignorance of his petitioners. At least the ambition manifests their deep attachment to him. However, he responds sharply when the other disciples (in whose minds the earlier question of who is the greatest remains unresolved) become indignant at John and James and their bid for authority and precedence within the band of disciples.

Jesus reminds them of the nature of earthly authority and of the despotic way it is exercised, and then bluntly commands,

'This is not to happen among you'. Discipleship of him means brotherhood among his disciples, and brotherhood means mutual service. He goes further. He sets himself as their example and names himself as the servant and ransomer of all. The authority they will have among those to whom they will preach Jesus is itself to be service.

'A servant,' Jesus says elsewhere, 'is not greater than his master, and it is enough for the servant to be like his master'. We servants are like Jesus (the Servant of God and men) only to the extent that we believe that as he came to serve so are we here, where we are in time and place, in order to serve. That must be our belief and we must act out of that belief and do so freely and out of love, acknowledging only one compulsion — that love of Christ which urges us, of which St Paul writes.

To his saying that he had come to serve, Jesus adds, 'and to give his life for all'. We, too, are to lay down our lives — our time, our talents, our hearts — in the service of others.

Second Week
Thursday
Luke 16:19-31

The parable of Dives and Lazarus illustrates the fact that our attitude to our neighbour in need manifests what is our real attitude to God himself. As John says, 'A man who does not love the brother that he can see cannot love God whom he has never seen'. The person who is blind to his neighbour in need, or hardens his heart against him, is thereby blinding himself to God and to those whom God has sent, and hardening his heart against God himself.

It is not that Dives act harshly towards Lazarus or is actively against God. It is simply that neither of them impinges on his consciousness or touches his heart. There is always hope for the persecutor of man and the hater of God; but indifference to either seems to breed, generally speaking, hardness of heart. For indifference to others usually implies a pre-occupation with self — a preoccupation which, given our finiteness, is ultimately shallow and, given its solitariness, necessarily sterile. John asks, 'If a man rich enough in this world's goods saw a brother in need but closed his heart to him, how could the love of God be living in him?' How much worse, then, is the state of one who does not even see a brother in need. Dives, by excluding Lazarus from his table, deserves to be excluded from the joy of the eternal feast of everlasting life.

He cannot enter the plea that he did not know these things, any more than we can. Dives had Moses and the Prophets with their messages of social justice and their exhortations to compassion and almsgiving. But he was as deaf to them as he was blind to Lazarus and heedless of God. When the heart is so hardened nothing can touch it, not even the sight of one risen from the dead — as Jesus will demonstrate in his own case.

We, too, can suffer the same fate. Though we have been 'clothed in purple', redeemed by the blood of Christ, and have 'fared sumptiously every day' on the Body and Blood of Christ, we are deservedly condemned if we do nothing for our brothers in need. The Eucharist is the abiding memorial of the love of Jesus who loved us and delivered himself up for us. The purpose of our sharing in it is that we, too, should be willing to live for, and to give of ourselves to others.

Second Week
Friday
Matthew 21:33-43, 45-46

There are few disappointments as piercing as seeing come to nothing a project in which we have invested time and effort and so much of ourselves. It is even worse when the project fails not because it iself was not feasible, or circumstances were against its succeeding, or through any fault of our own, but because of the malice of others. In such a situation, we can do one of two things: simply abandon it, or try to find some other way of bringing it to fruition. Such is the story of God's project of making all men citizens of his Kingdom.

One of the saddest laments in the Old Testament is found in Isaiah's 'Song of the Vineyard' (5:1-7). 'Let me sing to my friend the song of his love for his vineyard' — a love which led him to prepare the soil carefully, to plant choice vines, to protect it with hedge and watch-tower. But, 'sour grapes were all that it gave'. The disappointed vinegrower asks, 'What more could I have done for my vineyard that I have not done?' — and passes judgment on it. 'The vineyard of Yahweh Sabaoth is the House of Israel and the men of Judah, that chosen plant. He expected justice, but found bloodshed; integrity, but only a cry of distress.'

Jesus' hearers would understand this parable from the first word; and in the servants slain by the wicked vine-tenders, they would see the prophets of old, of whom Jeremiah had said (7:23-26): '. . . day after day I have persistently sent you all my servants, the prophets; but they have not listened to me . . .'

But God does not simply abandon his project: his judgment on faithless Israel includes the promise to the gentiles of admission into his Kingdom; and to effect this he finally sends his Son — even though he will be cast out of the vineyard and killed, crucified outside Jerusalem.

A condition of our membership in the Kingdom is that we bring forth the fruits which God rightly expects of us, that we be fruitful vines, not bearers of sour grapes. We cannot, as the wicked vine-dressers attempted to do, gain possession of the Kingdom by human reckoning or violence — except that violence of which Jesus says, 'The Kingdom of Heaven allows violence, and the violent carry it off'. But the violence of which he speaks is the hard line we must take against ourselves and our waywardness which is involved in the effort to do good and avoid evil.

Second Week
Saturday
Luke 15:1-3, 11-32

It is easy and healthily humbling for us to recognise our-selves in the younger, the prodigal, son. It is reassuring to know that the earthly father of the parable is, in his all-wrong-forgetting love, a true reflection of our heavenly Father. But it is the presence of the elder son which hones the point of the story. The real question is, How like the elder son am I?

The chapter of Luke's gospel from which this passage is taken begins with the adversaries of Jesus complaining that 'This man welcomes sinners'. Luke gives us Jesus' response, not at all a defence, in three parables of Jesus. A man loses then recovers a sheep — just one among many. He says to his neighbours, 'Rejoice with me'. A woman loses a small coin then recovers it — one among a few. She says to her neighbours, 'Rejoice with me'. A man looses the younger of his only two sons and regains him. He invites the older son to join him in rejoicing — and we are not told the other brother's final decision.

If the neighbours in the first and second instances declined to accept the invitation it would be, at the worst, mere churlish-ness and un-neighbourly behaviour. But in the third case, which is an image of Jesus' welcoming sinners, the response to the invitation is clearly much more serious. To refuse to rejoice in the return of a sinner points to self-righteousness on the part of the refuser — with all the wrongheadedness that this implies.

It may be felt that the older brother has a point. After all, his young brother had squandered much of the family's wealth, had shamed his father and brother by his dissolute life and had even stooped to becoming a tender of pigs. His homecoming was motivated not so much by familial love as material comfort. Why, then, should he rejoice in the prodigal's return?

But that is exactly the challenge offered by the parable: mercy, love and compassion know nothing of such reasoning as that of the elder brother. His complaints are irrelevant when the lost has been found.

Thus Jesus replies to his critics. Their attitude is that of the elder brother — an attitude wrong in itself because self-righteous and because it is incompatible with genuine love, and wrong in that it leads to a not easily cured spiritual sickness — a hard, embittered and angry heart.

Third Week of Lent

Third Sunday of Lent
Year A
John 4:5-42

Only John records this incident, Jesus' encounter with the Samaritan woman, the setting of which is so easily imagined, the drama of its unfolding so readily felt.

It is just on high noon. Jesus, on a three days' journey from Judea to Galilee is, naturally, tired and thirsty. Jacob's well, with its promise of refreshment, invites rest, and he gratefully takes it; for Jesus is fully human. He knew what it was to be tired; yet he himself is the eternal rest of souls, the maker and keeper of the promise, 'Come to me . . . and you will find your soul's rest' (Mt 11:28). He knew what it was to be thirsty — he who invites, 'If anyone is thirsty let him come to me and drink' (Jn 7:37).

One comes — a woman of Samaria, a territory interposing itself between Judea and Galilee. Traditionally, the Samaritans and Jews were mutually hostile, sometimes intransigently so (cf. Lk 9:51-56) but not universally: the disciples who have just left Jesus clearly expect to be sold food in the nearby town.

Here Jesus is delightfully unconventional. He is 'a Jew', as the Samaritan woman says, yet he asks to drink from her bucket. He is a Rabbi, as his returning disciples note, yet he is actually talking in public with a woman!

The Samaritan woman often gets a bad press. True, she is presently living with a man who is not her husband. But his five predecessors were husbands. Whether her many marriages terminated in death or in the then permissible divorce we simply do not know, and so it is quite unfair to regard her as a depraved person. Either case (a series of deaths or divorces) would account for her present man's reluctance to marry: superstition or fear if her previous husbands had died, the question of respectability and appearances if there had been a series of divorces. Whatever the truth, she would have to be, I think, a rather sad person.

She is by no means irreligious: she venerates the greatness of her people's ancestor, Jacob — is rather jealous for his honour, in fact; and she is firm in her belief in a Messiah to come (who, in her people's language was 'He Who Restores') and, even, rather wistful in her reference to him (v. 25).

She is by no means hardened in heart, and this despite the long years of lack of fulfilment in her personal history. She rapidly discerns something 'other', something special in Jesus, as her manner of addressing him indicates. In verse 9 it is, 'You, a Jew'; from verse 11 on it is, 'Sir'; in verse 19 she speculates (with simplicity, surely, as much as with the oft-asserted cynicism or defensiveness) that he is a 'prophet'; and finally, to her fellow townsfolk she speculates that he is in fact the Messiah.

This extraordinary growth in this woman's perception of Jesus is quite unforced. There is no miracle, no wonder performed which might dazzle or persuade. There are simply the words simply spoken by the Word and simply accepted by the woman as the truth.

But what words! He asks for water, but he offers a new gift of God. The former gift of God was the Law; but he will give the Spirit, the possession of whom means eternal life to those who receive him and the ability to give God the worship which he looks for — not outward observance but conversion of heart.

Moreover, Jesus reveals to her what he conceals from most: 'I who am speaking to you, I am he' — that Messiah of whose coming you have just spoken to me. And the woman does what no other has yet done — becomes a public witness to him, saying to her fellow citizens, 'I wonder if he is the Christ?'

In that great hymn, the *Dies Irae*, one verse begins with the line, 'Seeking *me* you sat down weary', recalling the scene we are presently contemplating. Each of us is the woman of Samaria. Daily, and all day, Jesus waits for us in loving ambush. In a muntiplicity of ways he will ask us to 'give'; constantly he will offer us his Spirit — possessing whom we rightly worship our Father and his, and so come to eternal life.

All that he requires of us is that, like the woman at the well, we have a teachable heart.

Third Sunday of Lent
Year B
Matthew 17:1-9

All four gospels tell of the occasion when Jesus drove the buyers and sellers out of the Temple but John does so at the greatest length and he alone includes such vivid details as Jesus' making and wielding a scourge of cords and his stampeding of the cattle and sheep.

At the time of his temptation in the wilderness Jesus refused Satan's suggestion that he make the Temple the scene of a spectacular sign, casting himself down from its topmost point. But now he does so, even while refusing to give such a sign as his enemies demanded. For the signs Jesus gives aim at confirming believers in their faith, and not at convincing sceptics. His signs are for those who have hearts to believe, not for those who have only eyes to see.

However, even for these his opponents, his words of this occasion ('Destroy this Temple and in three days I will rebuild it') were memorable enough. At his trial, false witnesses urged a garbled version of them against him; they were thrown up at him as a taunt as he lay dying on the cross; and his enemies, dimly and uneasily apprehending what his disciples realised only after the resurrection, had them in mind when they asked Pilate for guards for his grave.

What, by his action, is Jesus demonstrating? What sign is he giving?

He is serving notice that a completely new order of things is about to be inaugurated and that he himself is the source and abiding centre of that new order of things — as well as the fulfilment, not merely its destroyer, of the old.

When the Father sent his Son into the world, it is as if he had given him the order which Jesus himself gives here — 'Take these things out of here'. Concretely, 'these things' are the sacrificial animals, and the 'here' is the Court of the Gentiles at the Temple. What he is really driving out is the notion of exclusiveness and of the sufficiency of mere exterior observance in man's relationship with God.

The revelation which God had hitherto made had been thwarted in its two-fold purpose — to bring the sure hope of salvation to all men, and to spiritualise man's worship of God. Exclusiveness was contrary to God's will for he had declared through his prophet Isaiah, 'My house shall be called a house of prayer for all the people'; whereas the scene in today's reading took place in the Court of the Gentiles, to go beyond which was, for a gentile, to incur the death penalty. As regards mere outward observance, Jesus' driving out the sheep and cattle signifies that such observance is not the kind the Father 'looks for'. He is to be worshipped 'in spirit and in truth', as Jesus explained to the woman at the well of Jacob. Jesus' action causes his disciples to recall Psalm 68(69). The psalm is a lament by one persecuted on account of his zeal for the house of God, and a prayer for his vindication. The persecuted man asserts, also,

> I will praise the name of God with a song;
> I will extol him with my thanksgiving —
> more pleasing to the Lord than any ox or bull
> with horn and hoof.

With the coming of Jesus, the Temple and its worship came to both their fulfilment and their end, and this on three counts.

The Temple was the place of encounter between God and man, and 'the place where his glory dwelt'. Since in Jesus 'all the fulness of godhead was pleased to dwell', Jesus in his humanity becomes the sole necessary and sufficient Temple of God's dwelling among men and encountering men. Again, since Jesus is the Lamb of God he is the sole necessary and sufficient sacrifice for the taking away of the sin of the world. Finally, only Jesus through the gift of his Spirit can enable man to worship God in spirit and in truth.

Violence will be done to this new Temple, also; Jesus will be crucified. But his resurrection will not only vindicate his status as the true Temple of God among men it will also justify his actions on this occasion.

We who are members of Christ are, like him, temples of the divine indwelling. Hence St Paul writes (in 1 Cor 3:16-17),

Did you not realise that you were God's temple and that the Spirit of God was living among you? If anybody should destroy the temple of God, God will destroy him because the temple of God is sacred; and you are that temple.

To us also, then, Jesus says, 'Take these things out of here' — that 'exclusiveness' of ours whereby we will give of ourselves, in so many ways, to one and not to another, and that reliance of ours on, or making do with an exterior observance instead of striving after an ever deeper conversion of heart.

Third Sunday of Lent
Year C
Luke 13:1-9

Roughly speaking, by giving us as the gospel for the first Sunday of Lent that of the Temptation of Christ and, for the Second, that of the Transfiguration, the Church aims at establishing firmly in us the very basic general convictions of 'Present trial: future glory', and, 'No cross: no crown'. Cliches, no doubt, but also statements of actualities. Only from the Third Sunday on does the theme of the gospel reading vary from year to year.

Today's gospel is peculiar to St Luke, and is very nicely constructed. It stands complete in itself, unconnected with what goes before or follows, and is built up of three sections, each rounded off with the same refrain.

Some people bring to Jesus the news of Pilate's killing some fellow Galileans, inferring from their fate that they must surely have been great sinners. It is to this inference that Jesus responds, not to the news. They were no greater sinners than anyone else, Jesus says, and issues the warning, 'Unless you repent you also will perish'. Jesus then intensifies his affirmations. He recalls an even more bizarre incident, a pure accident, from which they would have drawn the same inference. Again Jesus denies the inference and again issues the warning, 'Unless you repent you also will perish'. Finally, Jesus tells a parable regarding an unfruitful tree; and his hearers are left to round off his words with the implied, 'Unless you bring forth fruit you also will perish'.

Jesus is concerned with something far deeper and more crucial than his hearers' rather silly notion that misfortune befalls people because of their sinfulness. It is not the dispelling of notions that Jesus is concerned with but a radical change of heart — repentance, and the bringing forth of fruits in keeping with that change of heart.

The parable embodying this concern of Jesus probably operates on two levels. On one level we may see the fig tree as representing Israel itself, still in need of a change of heart. The Prophets, John the Baptist, and Jesus himself, all sent in turn by God have urged a change of heart on the people; but, as a whole, Israel has not responded.

These, the parable says, are the last days. If the change of heart required of them by God does not take place, then the tree will be uprooted and another planted in its place. Or, as Jesus says at the conclusion of another parable with the same message, 'I tell you, then, that the Kingdom of God will be taken from you and given to a people who will produce its fruit' (Mt 21:33-46).

With the call of the Gentiles, we have become that people to whom the Kingdom of God has been given; but we receive it on the same condition — that we bring forth fruits worthy of our citizenship in such and so great a Kingdom. And the first of these fruits is repentance, a change of heart which ever more constantly, ever more fully turns us away from sin and from self and towards God and neighbour. Without this change of heart we also shall perish.

The God who requires this of us is neither ruthless nor exacting. On the contrary, he is enormously patient, coming now for three years seeking to find fruit, and willing to be swayed by the request for more time made of him by the man who looks after the vineyard — that is, Jesus himself, our Mediator with the Father. Yes, God is patient; but we must not presume of his patience any more than Jesus would presume on his Father's loving-care for him when he refused to cast himself down from the pinnacle of the Temple.

Again, God's insistence that we be fruitful is not in the nature of a demand or exaction. It is an act of creative love. A fruit tree which does not bear fruit is a tree not fulfilling its potentialities. It is an anomoly; a piece of nature gone wrong. It is as a sign that we are fulfilling our God-given potentialities for goodness and holiness of life that God looks to see in us the fruits of a change of heart. As Jesus says of us, 'I chose you and I commissioned you to go out and bear fruit, fruit that will last. It is to the glory of my Father that you should bear much fruit and so prove to be my disciples' (Jn 15:16, 18).

Since our Baptism is the sign that we have chosen to accept the summons to repent we can re-phrase the words, 'to bring forth fruits in keeping with that repentence', as, 'to live out the implications of our Baptism'. Hence, Vatican II directs that during Lent baptismal and penitential themes should go together.

It is in Baptism that we die to ourselves in order to live to Christ, that we put off our former selves and put on Christ, that we are grafted onto the one true Vine in order to live by his life and so bring forth the fruits of good works.

Third Week
Monday
Luke 4:24-30

From the verses immediately preceding today's reading we learn that when, in the synagogue at Nazareth, Jesus read the Good News as proclaimed in Isaiah 61:1-2 and announced that it was fulfilled in himself, he initially 'won the approval of all'. But doubt quickly set in: 'This is Joseph's son, surely'. Then, finally, the murderous anger of which we read in today's passage.

The approval lasts just so long as they listen to Jesus and not to what their own 'wisdom' suggests to them. The doubt sets in when they presume to judge Jesus according to that 'wisdom'. Hatred and murderous intent flood their hearts when, in contradiction of their prejudices and preconceptions, Jesus assures them that the Good News, and therefore a place in the Kingdom, is meant also for the Gentiles — instancing great prophets of the past and the mercies of God shown, through those prophets, to representatives of the gentile nations.

Against such pride as theirs and presumption (for they presume to know the purposes of God and to restrict his saving action) the grace of God is powerless and can bring about no change of heart; and the 'gracious words' which come from Jesus' lips fall on ears that refuse to hear.

They seize Jesus and hustle him out of the town, intending to inflict on him the death reserved for blasphemers. No doubt Jesus' mother is a witness, and the prophecy of Simeon, 'This child is ... destined to be a sign that is rejected', wrings her heart as she sees the first fruits of its fulfilment.

In their own words and actions they are fulfilling the words of the prophet whom they have just heard read; for Isaiah had proclaimed the universality of God's saving plan and had said of the Servant whom God would send to effect it, 'He was despised and rejected'. The whole incident, therefore, is a summary of the earthly life and mission of Jesus — proclamation, rejection, death.

Contemplating the whole terrible scene we see how great and how destructive a power is prejudice and preconception in the human mind and heart, and how it can rally even religious conviction to its wrongheadedness. And how prone to them we are! But if we are to know the will of God in our regard we must rid ourselves of them since, as he himself assures us, his ways are not our ways nor ours his; and when in his 'wisdom' Peter, in reference to Jesus' prediction of his own passion, said, 'Lord, this must not happen to you', Jesus rebuked him with, 'The way you think is not God's but man's'.

Third Week
Tuesday
Matthew 18:21-35

Today's theme (our response to which should be that petition in the Lord's Prayer, 'Forgive us . . . as we forgive . .') has already been met with in the readings for Tuesday of the first week of Lent and Monday of the second. Nor is it new even to the New Testament. In Sirach (Ecclesiasticus) chapter 28, we find lines such as these:

> Forgive your neighbour the hurt he does you; and, when you pray, your sins will be forgiven.
> If a man nurses anger against another, can he then demand compassion from the Lord?
> Showing no pity for a man like himself, can he then plead for his own sins?
> Remember the Covenant of the Most High, and overlook the offence.

That last verse is particularly important. When God our Lord makes his forgiveness of us dependent on our forgiveness of others, he is not offering a bribe to induce us to forgive our neighbour, nor is he uttering a threat. He is simply stating a fact: the Covenant he has struck with his people requires that we forgive as we are forgiven.

The Covenant which God had entered into with us is not a quid pro quo — not goods in exchange for services: 'Serve me, and I'll look after you'! No. The terms of the Covenant are, 'You shall be my people and I shall be your God': it is an invitation to that intimate friendship which we call love.

Love is unitive; it joins two as one. God's seriousness in this matter of his uniting us to himself if manifested first in his creating us, then in his making himself known to us, and, supremely, in his sending his Son to become, with us, a man like us in all things, except sin. Jesus, therefore, embodies in himself, is himself the new and everlasting Covenant; and his becoming man is the model for our striving to become like God who has made us his children.

'Forgive in order to be forgiven' expresses more than purpose, more than result. It expresses the ideal of unitive love which is the Covenant — to be like God. God loves; therefore, I love. God forgives; therefore, I forgive.

Doing so, we follow the way of Jesus who showed us how to be 'children of your Father in heaven who causes his sun to rise and his rain to fall upon the unjust and the just, alike' (Mt 5:45).

Third Week
Wednesday
Matthew 5:17-19

The theme of today's reading, fulfilment, is everywhere in the New Testament — just as, in our own lives, it is everywhere the ultimate aim in all we do. Here, Jesus claims to be himself the fulfilment of the Law and the Prophets, is claiming to be the One towards whom all God's revelation up until now has been directing man's gaze while enabling them to 'put their faith in the Christ before he came'. This was the purpose (and the glory) of the Law — 'to be our guardian until Christ came'. Of John the Baptist, Christ's herald, Jesus says, 'It was towards John that all the prophecies of the Prophets and of the Law were leading'; and again, 'Up to the time of John, it was the Law and the Prophets; since then, the Kingdom of God has been preached'; and John himself, pointing the way to Jesus, says, 'The time has come and the Kingdom of God is at hand'.

Just as God guided the whole dynamic of the history of Israel to its culmination in Christ, so does he guide (if we will co-operate) the whole of our personal, individual history not simply to an end but to a fulfilment. And that fulfilment is our achieving our full stature in Christ.

We achieve such growth by fulfilling the Law which Jesus puts before us by word and example. 'On these two commandments' (love of God and love of the neighbour), he says, 'hang the whole Law and the Prophets also'. And again, 'Always treat others as you would like them to treat you; that is the meaning of the Law and the Prophets'. Similarly St Paul: 'The whole of the Law is summarised in a single command, Love your neighbour as yourself' — what James calls 'the supreme law of scripture'. Paul again: 'If you love your fellow man you have fulfilled the Law, for love is the Law in all its fulness'; and again, 'You should carry one another's burdens and so fulfil the Law of Christ'.

Without growth there can be no fulfilment; and without love there can be no growth. Without love, we turn in upon our sole selves; it is in loving that we go out to others and, in doing so, grow in compassion, understanding, tolerance, patience, kindness, helpfulness — in all those qualities by which we measure a person's maturity and stature, and which can deepen only in relation to others. But we do this not simply for the sake of our human growth but because 'the love of Christ impels us', just as his love for us impelled him to demonstrate in his own person his words, 'A man can show no greater love than to lay down his life for his friends'.

Third Week
Thursday
Luke 11:14-23

Once, in his home town, Jesus taught the people in such a way that they were astonished, and asked one another, 'Where did this man, the carpenter's son, get this wisdom and these miraculous powers?' — and, finding no answer, they refused belief. The same question is raised in today's reading; but, more than refusing belief, Jesus' critics here blasphemously (and quite unintelligently, as Jesus points out in v. 18) accuse him of being in league with Satan. And yet the miracles themselves are not denied, because undeniable. In the incident at Nazareth, what is involved is pre-judgment, unfounded expectation; in this incident we see the evil that can come from a hardened heart.

Jesus points this out. The only possible explanation of his casting out devils is that he works 'through the finger of God'. His hearers cannot fail to remember the prelude to Israel's being delivered from enslavement in Egypt. When Moses and Aaron confront Pharoah with the demand to be allowed to leave the country they work a number of signs and wonders. Pharoah's magicians cannot match them, and declare, 'This is the finger of God'. But Jesus' hearers are like Pharoah: 'But Pharoah's heart was stubborn . . . He refused to listen.'

Recalling this situation of enslavement, Jesus points out the purpose of his own life — to free man from the power of the forces of evil. Man is a kingdom divided. He experiences civil war within himself — the struggle between good and evil, darkness and light, to have the mastery of him; and the world in which man lives is a spiritual battlefield between those same forces of good and evil. There are two kingdoms, each with its own banner and leader, at war until the end of time.

Jesus, however, also announces that the victory is already his. He is the stronger man who takes away the weapons the other relied on, and shares out his spoil. By faith in Jesus, by following Jesus, everyone can share in this victory.

Jesus also points out the seriousness and centrality of this struggle between good and evil, darkness and light — be it on the personal or the cosmic level: no truce is possible; neutrality is impossible; no other allegiance is possible if one would be victorious. 'He who is not with me is against me; and he who does not gather with me scatters.'

But we note those words, 'with me' — with him in whom, as St Paul says, I can do all things.

Third Week
Friday
Mark 12:28-34

Jesus is asked a question, and answers it: the love of God is the first imperative of true religion; but he immediately links that love with another — love of neighbour — so that the single love of a person's heart flows simultaneously in two directions, each corroborating and authenticating the other. (Cf. Second Week: Thursday.) Here Jesus says these are the two greatest commandments of the Law; elsewhere he will say that together they express the meaning of the whole Law and the Prophets also. (Cf. Third Week: Wednesday.)

In the fourth chapter of his first letter, John speaks of the love which must characterise one who believes that God is love and who claims to believe in Jesus as the revelation of God's love for us. Among other things he says, 'We are to love because he loved us first'. St Bernard notes that the reason for loving

God is God, and that in Jesus we are shown how we are to love both God and neighbour — with all our heart, with all our mind, with all our strength.

With all our heart: that is, he says, tenderly. It was the tenderness of God's love for us which impelled him (when man, by sin, had cut himself off irretrievably from God) to send his Son to restore us to friendship with our Father. We love tenderly in return when we try to deepen that friendship by speaking to God from our heart in prayer as a friend speaks to a friend, a child to its father. And we love our neighbour tenderly when we show him persevering forebearance.

With all our mind: that is, Bernard says, wisely. It was the wisdom of God's love for us which decreed that Jesus should experience hardships, rejection, betrayal and death; for not only does he thereby give us an example to follow, not only a consolation in our own bitter experiences, but also an assurance that nothing need come between us and God's love. (Cf. Romans 8:38-39.) We love wisely in return when we accept the will of God into our own lives with faith, even when understanding is impossible and acceptance difficult. Our love of neighbour is wise when it seeks only his good, and is prepared to forego everything rather than come between any person and God, or permit the same to happen to us.

With all our strength: that is, perseveringly. As in his death Jesus loved us to the end and thereby demonstrated that God's love for us knows no limits, so we, too, must persevere in a whole-hearted love of God even in our darkest moments; we must persevere in the love of neighbour despite any experience of indifference, ingratitude or rejection.

Third Week
Saturday
Luke 18:9-14

That final line, 'For everyone who exalts himself will be humbled, but the man who humbles himself will be exalted', also rounds off an earlier incident in Luke's gospel (14:7-11). There, a guest invited to a wedding feast presumes (not troubling himself to learn his host's arrangements) to take a place of honour (thereby showing his high opinion of himself in comparison with others). There we already see the ugly reality of pride, or arrogance: the position of the host is ignored; and equals, as fellow guests, are graded as inferiors.

In today's reading, Jesus shows us how that same attitude can easily overflow into our dealings with God. Prayer is an invitation from God which both Pharisee and Tax-collector accept. The Pharisee in the parable does not ask himself how he appears in God's eyes: he tells God his own view of himself. Worse, he tells God his view of the Tax-collector — with the implication that God must surely agree. The Tax-collector, however, simply acknowledges how he stands in the sight of God — 'a sinner' — and makes the appropriate response to that situation — 'be merciful to me'. No failure there to recognise who God is who has invited him to prayer; no comparison with others; no pointing to good works which he may have done (— and the almsgiving and prayers and fasting of the Pharisee were good works: Jesus does not dispute that).

Concluding this parable, Jesus makes an astonishing claim — that he knows God's judgment: 'I tell you: the Tax-collector went home, again at rights with God; the Pharisee did not'.

The supreme example, and model for all others, of the one who humbles himself and is exalted by God is Jesus himself. St Paul writes:

Let this mind be in you which was also in Christ Jesus. Always God by nature, he emptied himself to take to himself the condition of a slave; and, being as all men are, he humbled himself and became obedient unto death, even the death of the Cross. Wherefore God has highly exalted him and has given him a name which is above all names (Philippians 2: 5-11).

That is to say, beyond all self-effacing behaviour, beyond all acknowledgement of one's condition in the sight of God, the essence of humility lies in submission to the will of God and the service of one's fellow human beings. For we learn who and what we truly are only when our relationships with God and with others are as they should be.

Fourth Week of Lent

Fourth Sunday of Lent
Year A
John 9:1-41

John constructs and narrates this chapter, complete in itself, wonderfully well. The story begins simply enough when Jesus spontaneously cures a man blind from birth. Then however, the whole thing becomes increasingly complex when the enemies of Jesus move in.

The cure of the blind man is unusual in that it is not asked for either by the man himself or his family or friends. It is clear enough that Jesus performs this miracle in order to give concrete expression to his verbal correction of his disciples' wrong-headed notion that there is a causal link between physical misfortune and some individual's personal sin. Jesus flatly denies this, and then goes on to assert that, used properly, even misfortune or other disability can be turned to occasions wherein God's glory is manifested.

Here, also, the cure of the blind man is an appropriate sign that Jesus is the true light who enlightens every person who is born into this world. And all are born blind — lacking the grace of God and the light of faith. It is probably right, therefore, to find in the manner in which the cure is wrought an echo of the Genesis story of God's creating man from the clay of the earth. That is to say, enlightened by Christ, a person becomes what St Paul calls 'a new creature'.

The prominence of the word 'sent' is also most probably deliberate and, therefore, significant. Jesus 'sends' the blind man to a pool of water whose name, Siloam, means (as John here explains) 'sent'. There, the man comes to see. The symbolism is that, to come to the spiritual enlightenment of faith, we must come to Jesus, the one 'sent' by the Father.

What, it would seem, was meant by Jesus as a simple object lesson for his disciples is suddenly raised to a new pitch of significance. The astounding miracle causes great public interest. Since the enemies of Jesus can not deny that it had happened, the actual performance of the deed must be discredited. Jesus can not be a prophet, for he had broken the Sabbath in two ways: in making the clay, he was 'kneading'; in curing the man, he was practising medicine. This will be their line.

As a result, we have a number of great 'confrontation' scenes: the Pharisees and the man (twice); the Pharisees and the man's parents; the Pharisees and Jesus; and, finally, as climax — simple, serene yet intense — Jesus and the man, face to face.

Then there is the progressive revelation of the characters involved: the Pharisees, as their every move is frustrated, become more and more entrenched in their arrogance and in their hostility towards Jesus. The man becomes bolder and bolder, even provocative, in his replies to his inquisitors. The parents of the man display their caution, even timidity.

But the real progression is a spiritual one. We see how the man born blind comes first to physical sight and then to that spiritual sight which we call faith in Jesus.

The man's coming to faith is gradual — very like that of the woman at the well. As she progresses from, 'You, a Jew' to, 'Sir' then to, 'a prophet' and finally to, 'the Messiah', so this man progresses from, 'a man' to, 'a prophet' to, 'the Son of Man'.

In contrasting parallel, the Pharisees, who are not blind physically, become increasingly blind spiritually as their rejection of Jesus culminates in their expulsion of the man to whom Jesus has given both sight and faith. And since this blindness of theirs is wilful it is also culpable.

Thus the whole episode finally reveals its deepest meaning when Jesus says,

> I have come into this world so that sentence may fall on it, that those who are blind should see and those who see should become blind.

That is to say, Jesus' coming into the world results in the enlightenment of faith for those humble enough to accept him;

but it results in an even greater blindness for those who rely on a wisdom of their own. As Jesus says elsewhere, the Father reveals things to the little ones and conceals them from the self-wise.

The season of Lent is a time for especial striving to be counted among such little ones.

Fourth Sunday of Lent
Year B
John 3:14-21
With introductory, 'Jesus said to Nicodemus'

We read of the 'lifting-up of the serpent' in Numbers 21:4-9. In the wilderness, the people had murmured against Moses and had thereby brought upon themselves a visitation of deadly serpents. As Moses made intercession for the victims, 'the Lord bade him make a serpent of bronze and set it up on a staff, bringing life to all who should look towards it as they lay wounded'.

Later on, the up-lifted serpent became a symbol of salvation: we read in Wisdom 16:6-7, 'They had a symbol of salvation to remind them of the precept of your Law. For he who turned towards it was saved — not by what he saw but by you, the Saviour of all'.

In today's reading, Jesus foretells his being lifted up on the cross as the Saviour of all. But there is a difference between the bronze serpent on the staff in the desert and Jesus on the cross of Calvary. In the case of the serpent, a person was not saved 'by what he saw'; in the case of the crucified Jesus, a person is saved by what he sees with the eye of faith. For Jesus, crucified and risen, is the 'Saviour of all'.

This prediction of Jesus — that he would be 'lifted up' — he repeats: 'When you have lifted up the Son of Man, you will recognise that it is myself you look for' (Jn 8:28); and again, 'Yes, if I am lifted up from the earth, I will draw all men to myself', again foretelling his crucifixion as John there (12:32-33) notes.

The crucifixion of Jesus is the supreme proof of what follows: 'God so loved the world that he gave up his only-begotten Son, so that those who believe in him may not perish but have eternal life'.

In more than one of this sermons, Newman remarks on the Scriptures' habit of attributing human feelings to God, and notes that here, by the very words 'gave up', self-denial is attributed to God. He adds that 'this incomprehensible attribute of Divine Providence' is 'especially calculated to impress upon our minds the personal character of the Object of our worship'. For it is a characteristic of personal love (the love given by a person) that one will put oneself aside for the sake of another.

Lent is a time for self-denial — which is not only giving up things pleasing to oneself, but is the giving-up of the self itself — self-will, self-seeking, self-indulgence, self-centredness. During Lent we try to approach still nearer to that self-denial of which St Paul speaks when he says, 'I live — now not I but rather Christ lives in me'.

'God so loved the world that he gave up his only-begotten Son so that those who believe in him may not perish but have eternal life.' These words have, aptly, been called a summary of the whole Gospel, the Good News that God loves mankind and has destined it for eternal life. Love is not simply an attribute of God as is, say, 'majesty'. God's love for man is not simply a kindly regard for man; it is active in man's history. God loves man; and therefore good things happen to man. He gives up his only Son in order to bestow sonship of himself on all mankind; for his is a love which embraces the whole world.

The absolute reversal of man's fate once God intervenes is well captured by the words, 'not perish but have eternal life'. To perish and to live are total opposites. Through God's sending his only Son into the world, man who was, because of sin, faced with first temporal and then eternal death (the 'second death' of Revelations 2:11) now has eternal life offered him for the taking. It is an offer, however, which he is free to reject. For, as Jesus says here, it is possible for man to prefer darkness to light, prefer to perish rather than to have life.

Lent is a time for discerning more closely our personal preferences.

Fourth Week of Lent
Year C
Luke 15:1-3, 11-32

We have just read the well-known 'mercy' parable of The Prodigal (or Lost) Son, prefaced by the introductory verses to this whole chapter of Luke's gospel.

What to us is something which irresistibly draws our hearts to Jesus was, for a sector of the people of his time, a cause for complaint: 'This man welcomes sinners and eats with them'. Luke records this attitude, and then gives us three parables in which Jesus tells his critics that their attitude is wrong, and that they should, in fact, rejoice that he is so loving towards the outcasts of a self-righteous society.

The three parables are The Lost Sheep, The Lost Coin, The Lost Son; and they have the common theme of God's joy at recovering what had been lost to him — a joy which others, who have themselves not suffered the loss, are invited to share.

It is the issuing of this invitation which makes the Prodigal Son parable something much more than a vividly written assurance of God's mercy towards those who turn to him through a conversion of heart. If that were all that the parable was intended to convey then the introduction of the older brother in the opening words would be superfluous, and the story would end with the words, 'And they began to celebrate'.

It is the presence of the older brother which raises the real challenge for Jesus' hearers. Will they join in rejoicing with God and his angels over the repentence of a sinner, and welcome his as a brother?

In the parable, this is also the question which the older brother must face and answer; and the parable is both dramatic and disturbing in that we do not know its outcome in this crucial respect.

Perhaps it may be felt that the older brother has a justifiable grievance. After all, the younger son did squander a large part of the family fortune, had shamed his father and brother by his profligate life and, even more, by his stooping to become a tender of pigs, and had come home only because, whatever his father's reception of him, he could only be better off than he was.

But that is precisely the challenge issued by the parable. Mercy, love, compassion know nothing of such reasoning. All that the older brother urges is irrelevant when the lost is found and the dead has come back to life.

Hearing the party noises as he approaches home, the older brother does not simply go inside and ask what is going on. He summons a servant and asks him — and is angry at what he finds out. His father goes out to him, literally and metaphorically. The older son is merely rude. He does not give him the name 'father', and addresses him angrily and abruptly. Worse, he reduces their relationship to a crass quid pro quo: 'I have slaved for you, obeyed you always; and you have not once rewarded me'. There is no acknowledgement of his father's love for him, no demonstration of love for his father. He does worse. He will not call the prodigal 'brother'; it is, hurtfully to his father and contemptuously of his brother, 'This son of yours'. Deeply hurt but, even more, deeply anxious over his older son's hardness, the father can only gently insist on the superior claims of love — both fatherly and brotherly.

This, then, is the warning Jesus is giving his critics: their attitude is that of the older brother; and that attitude is wrong in itself, because incompatible with genuine love, and productive of one of the less easily healed of all spiritual ailments — a hard, embittered and angry heart.

The suitability of this gospel to the Season of Lent is evident. Lent is a season of summons to repentence. It is a call to us to do as the prodigal son did — to come to our senses and to return to our Father. Or, if like the older son we have never left home, the gospel reminds us that that does not entitle us to sit in judgment on those who have and who have returned home.

To refuse to rejoice in their homecoming is to commit the ultimate folly, for it is tantamount to saying that God's love and mercy are wrong.

Fourth Week
Monday
John 4:43-54

John himself, in narrating this incident, invites us to recall Jesus' earlier miracle at Cana which he relates in chapter 2 of his gospel and which he calls 'the first of the signs given by Jesus'. That 'sign' was Jesus' changing water into wine — signifying the coming of a new order of things. Here, today, the miracle is salvation from bodily death — signifying Jesus' power, and mission, to save mankind from spiritual death. And each of these sign-miracles takes place, as John notes, on a 'third day'. Thus John directs our attention to the still-in-the-future resurrection of Jesus — which, above all, manifests his power over both physical and spiritual death and his power and mission to 'make all things new'.

As at the wedding feast at Cana (and indeed as elsewhere — for example in the case of the Syro-Phooenician woman in

Mk 7:24-30) so here we have Jesus apparently refusing a request. However, his words are not a refusal but an invitation to faith; and on both occasions the invitation is accepted: after the changing of the water into wine 'his disciples believed in him', while here, 'he (the court official) and all his household believed'. Whatever Jesus does in our lives has the same purpose — to elicit what should be our constant protestation and prayer: 'Lord, I believe. Help my unbelief.'

The court official was already in Cana, presumably on the king's business, when Jesus arrived there. He does not come to Cana in order to seek Jesus but, hearing of Jesus' arrival, he seizes the opportunity. In anyone who comes to us in need of any kind, Jesus comes. It is up to us to seize the opportunity that Jesus thus gives us of serving him in serving others. Again, assured that his son will live, the official does not straightway rush off back to Capernaum to see for himself his son restored to health. It is only the next day that he learns of his son's recovery. This delaying on his part is sometimes said to be a demonstration of his faith. More likely, I think, it was simply that the business which had brought him to Cana had not yet been completed.

It is an illustration of a practical point. Jesus' action in our lives will not be in conflict with the duties of our state in life. Indeed, the faithful fulfilment of our duties and obligations, since these are usually towards others, can be our most constant service of Jesus himself.

Fourth Week
Tuesday
John 5:1-3, 5-16

Like the miracle recounted yesterday, the one of which we have just read constitutes a sign of spiritual resurrection. Just as Jesus has power to save from physical sickness and, even, death, so he has power to save from spiritual sickness and death. Jesus himself makes this clear when, meeting the man later in the Temple, he urges him to conversion of heart — to break with sin and to turn wholeheartedly to God. Failure to do so is more death-dealing than any disease.

This reading, therefore, recalls to our minds the whole purpose of Lent — the deepening of our change of heart as we prepare to celebrate the passion and death of Jesus, through which we are freed from sin, and his resurrection, which is the sign and guarantee of our own.

In contrast with the miracle of which we read yesterday, there is no request made of Jesus to work a miracle nor, on Jesus' part is there a demanding of faith. Jesus takes the initiative by spontaneously asking the sick man if he wishes to be cured. The sick man thinks purely in terms of the healing powers attributed to the waters of the pool. When the Samaritan woman at the well showed the same lack of understanding, Jesus instructed her. Here, however, he simply commands the sick man to get up and walk.

The sick man evidently had faith. He immediately obeys Jesus; and, in taking up his mattress (it being the sabbath day) he acknowledges Jesus' authority over the sabbath. When he is rebuked by the religious leaders for breaking the sabbath he defends himself by pointing out that to obey such authority as his healer had just shown can not be wrong. But, as we see so often in the gospels, when the heart is hardened the mind is closed even to such evidence of more than human authority and power. The only interest the religious leaders show is to try to find out who commanded this breach of the sabbath rest.

When the healed man himself finds out the name of the one who cured him he tells the authorities. There is in this no suggestion of beytrayal or malice. He is simply answering a question put to him by his acknowledged religious leaders. What would be a betrayal of Jesus and of the marvel worked by him would be his failing to heed Jesus' words, 'Be sure not to sin any more' — words we rightly take to be addressed to us also as we recall the great things Jesus has done for us and at what cost to himself.

Fourth Week
Wednesday
John 5:17-30

Today's reading takes up where yesterday's left off. Yesterday, Jesus, in his opponents' view, himself broke the Sabbath by healing a sick man, and, by ordering that man to carry away his mattress, had caused that man, also, to violate the Sabbath.

The matter was not trivial. By claiming to be master of the Sabbath, by asserting that the Sabbath was made for man and not vice versa, and by, time and again, 'working' (cf. Mt 12:1-8, 9-14. Lk 13:10-17; 14:1-6. Jn 7: 20-24; 9:1-41) on the Sabbath Jesus was, in his enemies' eyes, a law breaker with no regard for God to whom the Sabbath belonged exclusively. Jesus tells them that, in fact, God never ceases to be at work in his creation and that he himself, therefore, must do the same since he is his Father's son.

God is active in his creation of things, active in the control of the world, active in the redemption of the world. He dwells in the elements, giving them existence; in the plants, giving them growth; in the animals, giving them sensation; and in each of us, giving us existence, growth and sensation, enabling us to perceive him in the things which he has made and, by the inpouring of his Spirit, making us his temple and his dwelling-place.

This reading today is an assertion of the co-equal divinity of the Son with the Father: 'Whatever the Father does the Son also does'; 'As the Father gives life, so the Son gives life'; 'Whoever refuses honour to the Son refuses honour to the

Father'. The activity, the giving of life, the judgment of the Father and the Son are identical, because they are one in love, one in will. There exists between the Father and the Son a most perfect union of mind and heart. 'My food,' Jesus said, 'is to do the will of the one who sent me' (Jn 4:34); and again, 'My aim is to do not my own will but the will of him who sent me' (Jn 5:30); and again, 'I have come down from heaven not to do my own will but the will of him who sent me' (Jn 6:38).

Through his gift of the Holy Spirit, who enables us to have faith in Christ and thereby become one with Christ, God our Father has made us his sons also. Such is his love for us. In return, we show our love for him and show ourselves to be true sons of his by seeking his will for us and, like Jesus, doing it.

Fourth Week
Thursday
John 5:31-47

Again, today's reading takes up where yesterday's left off. Yesterday's assertion of the oneness of Jesus with his Father is followed by today's assertion that, variously, John the Baptist, Jesus' own works (and, through them, the Father himself) and the Old Testament scriptures all bear witness to the fact that Jesus is the One who was to be, and who has been, sent by the Father so that we, believing in him, might have life through him.

But each witness is, in turn, rejected by Jesus' hearers. John was a lamp, alight and shining, to draw the people's attention to Jesus. But they would not heed John. The works which Jesus does (which are also his Father's works) they refuse to see for what they are — signs which show who Jesus is and what his mission. (See Fourth Sunday, Year A.) They read the scriptures, but fail to see that the Law and the Prophets point to, and come to their fulfilment in, Jesus.

The reason for all this blindness is that they look for approval from one another, and care nothing for God's approval. To seek the approval of men is not wrong in itself, for we must do our best to avoid giving offence. (Cf. 2 Cor 6:37.) It becomes wrong when we rate it, and the self-assurance it brings, higher than seeking the approval of God and the self-abandonment to his will which this necessitates. Proud of their observance of the Law of Moses, they are not alert to the One whom Moses foretold would come and to whom they were to listen (cf. Deut 18:15). And so Moses, the People's great intercessor (cf. Ex 32:11-14: First Reading) before God, will become their accuser. Priding themselves on their investigations of the scriptures and their own interpretations of them, they have not heard the voice of God speaking through those very scriptures. God's word finds no home in them; and when the Word was made flesh and lived and moved among them, his own people did not accept him — a rejection which is soon to culminate in his crucifixion.

Today's reading warns us that a closed mind is all too easily followed by a closing of the heart. It warns us that prejudices and preconceptions as to how God ought to act in our lives all too readily blind us to the fact that he actually does act in our lives — or would act if our minds and hearts were open to him.

Fourth Week
Friday
John 7:1-2, 10, 25-30

Just before today's reading takes up at verse 25, Jesus had warned his hearers: 'Do not keep judging by appearances'. Several times in the course of our Lenten readings we have seen Jesus' hearers doing exactly that — and thereby completely misinterpreting his words and his works. So, too, here. While it was known that the Messiah would be descended from David and would be born in Bethlehem it was also thought by some that, having been born, he would be hidden in some secret place until the day of his appearing. Hence, they decided, Jesus could not be the great Deliverer since his life was an open book. In part, they were right: they knew where he came from in his earthly existence; but his heavenly existence as the eternal Son of the Father was hidden from them.

Jesus agrees with them: Yes, they know all about his earthly origins; but they misinterpret the 'hiddenness' of him — fail to perceive the divinity of him. Instead of passing, by faith, through Christ-Man in order to come to Christ-God (and, thereby, come to the Father with whom he is one) they judge by appearances. They regard only the man; and therefore do not have the knowledge of the Father which can be attained only through him; for as Jesus says elsewhere, 'No one knows the Father except the Son and anyone to whom the Son chooses to reveal him'.

The human nature of Jesus was not a mask put on to conceal his divinity; it was a reality which, through his works, was to reveal his divine origins. Since his hearers judge by appearances, they reject his claim that he comes from the Father, of whom he claims to have unique knowledge; and, rejecting his claim, they wish to arrest him as a blasphemer.

And so it continues. Many of our contemporaries can admire Jesus' life and teaching and, even, shape their own lives by that teaching; but they will not say with St Thomas, 'My Lord and my God!'

That fatal flaw of judging by appearances can all too easily be found in us also — not in relation to Jesus, perhaps, but in the way we regard ourselves and others. It is easy to fall into the habit of a routine observance of the externals of our faith without making much effort to grow in the Spirit. It is also very easy to judge others simply on appearances and fail to see the Christ in them.

Fourth Week
Saturday
John 7:40-52

As yesterday's, so today's reading involves: a discussion concerning the origin of the Messiah; the desire of some to do violence to the person of Jesus; and their impotence to do so until he himself permits it — when the 'hour', of which he several times speaks, finally comes. Again the question is raised: Who is this man? As always, the discussion of that question results in deep divisions: 'the people could not agree'. Some wondered if he were not, perhaps, the Messiah. 'Some would have liked to arrest him.' Some, like the Temple police, are impressed but bewildered. Some, like Nicodemus, speak up for a judicious neutrality. Finally, some, the authorities, are confirmed in their opposition — based, as has been seen before, on ignorance, and on the unshakeable assurance which their own partisan reading of the Scriptures gives them.

'Never,' said the Temple police, 'has anybody spoken as this man'. For 'The Word of God is something alive and active: it cuts like any double-edged sword, only more finely'. The result of Jesus' speaking is always division — according as his words are accepted or rejected. He himself had said that, as a result of his coming, households would be divided (and, indeed, the whole of humanity) — not necessarily in charity but in faith, according as people believed in him or not.

The issue is not confined to that particular time, is not simply an issue for the contemporaries of Jesus. Today is the time of Jesus' presence among us. Through the proclaiming of the Gospel, Jesus' words are addressed to us here and now. And so the words of Jesus still cause division. But the division to which we must chiefly attend is the division within ourselves. He himself said, 'Happy are they who hear the word of God — and keep it'. Hearing the word is not enough; admiration of the speaker is not enough. His words have to become the principles by which we lead our lives.

Another kind of self-division of which Jesus elsewhere warns us (in the parable of the Sower) is seen in his putting before us the case of the person who initially hears the word with enthusiasm but falls away in time of trial; or the case of the person who accepts the word, but allows the cares of this world — ambitions of various kinds — to assume an importance greater than that of nurturing the Word which Jesus the Sower has sown.

Fifth Week of Lent

Fifth Sunday of Lent
Year A
John 11:1-45

In the first reading we have God promising to bring the People of Israel back out of exile to their own homeland. For such an event (humanly speaking unlooked-for, impossible) the resurrection of dead bones to living life is the only symbol, image, 'prophecy' that Ezechiel can find.

In the gospel, Lazarus is even more of an exile than the exiled People — for he is physically dead. Jesus raises him from the dead. In Lazarus, therefore, the symbol of the prophecy becomes a physical reality. But this actual raising of Lazarus from the dead is itself, on a higher level, another symbol — a sign, an irrefutable demonstration that God is active in human lives and history, and that his action has as its end the raising of man from spiritual death to eternal life through Christ Jesus our Lord.

The symbolic aspect of the actual raising of Lazarus has particular relevance to this season of Lent in which we, relying on Jesus our Lord, hope and strive to rise out of ourselves, our past, and our present, ever more fully, in order to live no longer for ourselves but for him who died and, yes, rose again for us — as St Paul writes and the Eucharistic Prayer quotes.

This going out of ourselves, this dying to self and to all self-love, is the commission given us by Jesus when he says we must take up our cross every day. Our Lenten effort is simply an intensification of a year-round, life-long striving. In this season, as St Leo the Great says, 'what every Christian should always be doing must now be performed more earnestly and devoutly'. In today's gospel, St Thomas the Apostle, uncomprehending but loving totally, says, 'Let us go, too, that we may die with him' — indicating that death with Jesus is better than life without him. His words should be ours also.

Arrived at Lazarus' grave and having commanded that it be unsealed, Jesus prays — not in petition nor asking to be heard, but to convince the bystanders of the unceasing communication which exists between him and his Father. His prayer is also a reminder to the bystanders that he is not simply a wonder-worker nor his miracles simply wonders. They are signs that the Father, through his Son Jesus, is actively at work bringing salvation to mankind.

Jesus had already said, 'The hour is coming, and now is, when the dead will hear the voice of the Son of God, and those who hear will live' (Jn 5:25). Now he demonstrates the truth of that claim. He issues his command, and the dead man is immediately there, standing before all — still bound by the tokens of death but not by its bonds.

So it is with us through our hearing the voice of the Son of God. We, who must die, have already been freed from death. Physical death is, so to speak, the sacrament of sin — the visible sign that we have sinned, and the seal which would, were sin to prevail, make permanent our separation from God which sin entails. Jesus' raising of Lazarus proclaims, by this triumph over physical death, that he has also triumphed over the reality of which it is a sign — sin.

But before he prayed, Jesus wept — he who, in the resurrection of the dead, 'will wipe away every tear from their eyes'.

He weeps out of sheer compassion for the grief of others, and out of the sharpness of his own loss: 'for Jesus loved Martha and her sister and Lazarus'. Newman remarks that Jesus wept

> from spontaneous tenderness, from the gentleness and mercy, the encompassing loving-kindness and exuberant affection of the Son of God for his own work, the race of man. Their tears touched him at once, as their miseries had brought him down from heaven. His ear was open to them, and the sound of weeping went at once to his heart.

This is the heart, clearly well-known to them, that the sisters of the dying man appealed to when they sent Jesus the simple message, 'Lord, he whom you love is sick'. Clearly, they are doing more than inform Jesus of a fact; but there is no specific petition to him to act, still less to act in a particular way. They leave everything to him. So, too, had Mary his mother at the wedding feast at Cana simply said to him, 'They have no wine'. Whereupon, Jesus worked the miracle which John calls 'the first of his signs'.

This, too, is the heart to whom we appeal when we present ourselves before him for healing, or our lives for them to be transformed by him.

Fifth Sunday of Lent
Year B
John 12:20-23

In a striking way, the gospel story of the infancy of Jesus rehearses the story of his public life and the Paschal Mystery of his passion and resurrection.

Taken to the Temple, there to be presented to the Lord, Jesus is announced by Simeon to be destined to be 'a sign of contradiction for the rise and fall of many in Israel'. In the persons of the Magi, the gentiles come to him to acknowledge his sovereignty; and their coming is the signal for Herod to resolve on Jesus' death. The persecution of Jesus begins. The Holy Family take refuge in Egypt until, in a new Exodus, Jesus the new Israel returns home. 'Out of Egypt I have called my Son,' says Hosea of the ancient Israel and Matthew of the new.

In his public life, Jesus often asserts that acceptance or rejection of him constitutes a 'judgment' whereby a person is left either in light or darkness (e.g. Jn 3:19) has life or perishes (e.g. Jn 3:16, as well as throughout today's reading). Similarly, he says he comes to bring a sword, not peace (Mt 10:34) and to divide families. He is, the Apostle says, the cornerstone, yet rejected by the builders, and his cross is, to the Jews, a stumbling block, and, to the Greeks, mere folly.

The coming of the Gentiles to 'see' him (that is, to believe in him) signals that the 'hour' has come in which he will be 'lifted up' — first on the cross, and then into glory after he has accomplished his own personal Passover preceeding his Exodus from this world back to his Father.

The Greeks desire to see Jesus. In his lifetime, many saw Jesus; but few saw him with eyes of faith which saves. Evidently, these strangers, like the Magi, are among the first to fulfil the prophecy of Isaiah, 'The gentiles will put their trust in his name'; they are among the first of the 'other sheep' Jesus says he must gather into one only fold.

Jesus' reply to Andrew and Philip when they tell him of the Greeks' request is abrupt and startling: 'Now the hour has come' — that 'hour' of his death and glorification. At Cana he had said, 'My hour has not yet come'. During his public life he was immune from his enemies 'because his hour had not yet come'. But now, 'Now the hour has come'.

The similitude of the grain of wheat which Jesus then proposes explains the nature of his glorification. First he must die — but only in order to communicate to multitudinous others a share in the fulness of life which is in him as the Word made flesh, God become man. He will fulfil the promise of, demonstrate the truth of Isaiah's words, 'If he offers his life in atonement, he shall see his heirs . . .' As St Augustine says,

He himself was the grain that had to be made to die and to be multiplied — to be made to die by the unbelief of the Jews, to be multiplied by the belief of all the nations.

Jesus, therefore, will demonstrate in his own self this similitude of the single grain; and he immediately serves notice that what transpires in him must also be reproduced in his followers — of whom he is the Head to them the members, of whom he is the Christ to them who are Christians, other Christs. 'Wherever I am,' he says, 'my servant will be there, also' — ultimately in the glory of the Father, but first in the agony of the Passion.

Lent is especially the season when we examine ourselves to see to what extent we are willing to let the shadow of the cross fall upon our lives — even, as St Paul says, to be willing to be 'with Christ nailed to the cross'.

This vivid realisation by Jesus of what he must go through before he enters into his glory 'troubles' his soul: and so we have here John's equivalent of the other gospels' Agony in the Garden.

All the elements are there: distress of soul; the cry regarding the possibility of being delivered from the 'hour' or the 'cup'; the submission to the Father's will; the strengthening from heaven. It is rewarding to read these verses 27-29 together with the accounts of the Agony in Gethsemane in Matthew 26:36-46 or Mark 14:32-46 or, in particular, Luke 22:39-46.

Finally, Jesus utters a warning. His coming into the world, as the Light of the world, leaves us with only one fundamental choice — to choose the Light or to prefer the darkness.

Lent is a time for carefully discerning the choices we make in our daily lives.

Fifth Sunday of Lent
Year C
John 8:1-11

Of the gospel reading set down for today (the story of the woman taken in adultery) Raymond Brown, in his commentary on it, writes:

> No apology is needed for this once independent story which has found its way into the Fourth Gospel and some manuscripts of Luke, for in quality and beauty it is worthy of either locali- sation. Its succinct expression of the mercy of Jesus is as delicate as anthing in Luke; its portrayal of Jesus as the serene judge has all the majesty that we expect of John. The moment when the sinful woman stands confronted with the sinless Jesus is

one of exquisite drama, a drama beautifully captured in Augustine's terse Latin formula: Relicti sunt duo, misera et misericordia.

Two are left: a pitiable woman and Pity.

And the delicate balance between the justice of Jesus is not condoning the sin and his mercy in forgiving the sinner is one of the great gospel lessons.

Brown's opening words relate to the history of this passage's being, rather late in time, accepted into the canon of Christian scripture, an interesting history which may be read in any significant commentary on John's gospel. It is not surprising that it appears in some manuscripts of Luke's gospel: the story is so in keeping with others found in that 'Gospel of Mercy'. Most manuscripts, however, preferred to put it in John. Put where it is, it serves, as it were, as a concrete illustration of what would follow in that same chapter about 'evidence', 'testimony', 'judgment' and 'witnesses' — especially in regard to Jesus himself.

But all that is not relevant to our purpose here: 'mercy' and 'judgment' are.

In the intentions of its initiators, at least, this is an ugly scene. Jesus' enemies ask their question of Jesus 'as a test': they are laying a trap, 'looking for something to use against him'; and they simply use an unfortunate woman, publicly parading her, as a means to that end. They are, therefore, merely cynical when they address Jesus as 'Master'.

Clearly, from the confidence of their assertions, the case is open and shut, the facts irrefutable. It is so watertight (to prove adultery, eyewitnesses were necessary) that some commentators have suggested that the woman (wife, or at least bethrothed) was actually 'set up' by her husband or intended. Maybe so: but simply their use of this person as an instrument of their unworthy purposes is repellent enough.

The nature of the trap set for Jesus is familiar — a dilemma. 'Moses, in the Law, commanded us . . .' If Jesus demurs then he is not upholding the Law. If he assents to the stoning, then he is flouting the decrees of the occupying Roman authority.

If he demurs, he is not standing by Moses; if he assents, his practice of 'welcoming sinners and eating with them' is a sham.

It was a trap Jesus was not unfamiliar with. There was that matter of paying tax to Caesar — when Jesus said, in effect, 'The coin has Caesar's likeness stamped on it: it is his, therefore; so give it to him. You are made in the image of God; therefore, give yourselves to him to whom you belong.'

The question is put to him. Jesus squats and begins 'writing on the ground with his finger'. Or is he just doodling in the dust? Or is he, as has been conjectured, indicating various points of that very Law which his adversaries have just appealed to? Or is he simply expressing his revulsion at their whole proceedings?

Finally, as they urge the dilemma upon him, Jesus says, 'If any one of you has not sinned, let him be the first to throw a stone at her'. He is not saying that the Law may be enforced only by the sinless — for no man is. He is saying that proneness to condemnation of others springs from self-righteousness (real or imagined) but not from that righteousness which is of God. For God's action in a person moves him to show that mercy which is characteristic of God, moves him to prefer to suffer on the sinner's account, as Jesus will, rather than to condemn.

Jesus has lifted the question far above 'the letter of the Law which kills' to 'the spirit which gives life'.

It is helpful to visualise the whole scene. The noisy, self-important, self-assured entrance of the accusers, the shamed woman among them; the 'set' — they on one side, Jesus on the other, and the woman 'standing there in full view'. There is a brief dialogue, and suddenly the very minor figures in the dramatis personae, with studied casualness, melt away, so that the stage is occupied solely by the sinner and Jesus in confrontation: 'a pitiable woman and Pity'.

Always, this is our situation; but especially so in the season of Lent, the season of repentance and of change of heart. Always, Jesus' word to us in our repentance is, 'I will not condemn you; but sin no more'. Nor does he ever command what is impossible to fulfil.

Fifth Week
Monday
John 8:1-11 *See Fifth Sunday Year C*
Alternative reading for this day when yesterday was Year C: John 8:12-40

The Psalmist's prayer, 'Lord, send forth your light and your truth', was answered in a manner beyond all imagining when God the Father sent his Son into the world — the Son who is the true Word of God and who is God from God, Light from Light. The Psalmist's further prayer, 'Let that light and that truth be my guide', was superabundantly answered when the Word made flesh, Jesus, assured us, 'I am the Light of the world; anyone who follows me will not be walking in the dark, but will have the light of life'.

In our pilgrimage through our life on earth to our eternal life and promised home, Jesus is to us what the pillar of fire in the darkness was to the Israelites in their Exodus out of exile in Egypt to their homecoming in the Promised Land. Jesus is, says John, 'the true light who gives light to everyone born into this world'; and Simeon, at the presentation of Jesus in the Temple, announces him to be 'the light that will give light to the nations' — in fulfilment of the words of Isaiah, 'I will make you the light of the nations so that my salvation may reach to the ends of the earth'. And Jesus is, as he himself said, not only Guide and Leader, but also the Way itself. (Thus all the way to heaven *is* heaven.) He is, also, he says, the Truth — to know whom is to have life; and he himself is the life in which we are meant to share, for, he says, 'I have come that they may have life and have it to the full'.

If it is by his life that we live, then we should (in some way) be recognisably the kind of person he was, and fulfil (in some way) the mission in life that was his. So he himself commands. He who called himself the Light of the world told his followers, 'You are the light of the world'; and he gave them their mission, 'Let your light so shine that people, seeing your good works, may give glory to your Father in heaven', the Light which suffers no overshadowing.

We prove ourselves light, our light shines, when, as the Peace Prayer of St Francis puts it, where there is hatred, we sow love; where there is injury, we sow pardon; where doubt, faith; where despair, hope; where sadness, joy.

Fifth Week
Tuesday
John 8:21-30

The controversy over who Jesus is continues; and Jesus again warns his hearers of the shortness of the time left to them in which to accept him. He warns them again that acceptance or rejection of him is a matter of life or death. As they then, so we here and now, have the choice — to be 'from below' or 'from above', to be 'of this world' or not 'of this world'.

To be 'from below', or to be 'of this world', is to be earth-bound in our aspirations, to be unwilling to live in the Spirit, to make ourselves the centre of our lives — in short, to be everything that Jesus himself was not, and expects his followers not to be. So he prayed to his Father regarding his disciples, 'They are not of this world any more than I am of this world'. And Paul reminds the Corinthians, 'Instead of the spirit of the world (by which he means self-centredness, self-indulgence) we have received the Spirit that comes from God'.

Jesus tells his unbelieving hearers that he will give one final sign — his crucifixion and glorification. His death will be at their hands: 'When you have lifted up the Son of Man', on the cross; his glorification will be his Father's doing: 'He accepted death on the cross. Therefore God has highly exalted him, and has given him the name which is above all names.'

Jesus had earlier referred to his being 'lifted up', and would do so again a few days before his death saying, 'When I am lifted up from the earth, I shall draw all things to myself'. The image of the crucified Christ is at the heart of our Christian faith, for it is the supreme evidence that 'He loved me, and delivered himself up for me'; and the Christian 'glories only in the cross of our Lord Jesus Christ through whom the world is crucified to me and I to the world'.

'Whoever wishes to be a follower of mine,' Jesus says, 'must take up his cross daily and follow me.' We, too, in some way, must join Jesus in being 'lifted up' in the acceptance of whatever pain or suffering or loss God permits to befall us. But we do so in the firm faith that that being lifted up is simply a prelude to our being lifted up into, and glorified in, eternal life with God.

Fifth Week
Wednesday
John 8:31-42

Jesus sometimes speaks of his word finding a home in us. Here he speaks of our finding a home in his word: 'If you make my word your home, you will indeed be my disciples'. The two expressions, perhaps, come to the same thing in the end; but the difference is worth noting.

When he speaks of his word finding a home in us, Jesus lays on us the onus of accepting or rejecting his word — that is to say, his claims, his message, his teaching, his Law. These things come to us as a would-be guest, so to speak. It is up to us to give them a hospitable welcome — by accepting them in faith, and, out of love, making Jesus' word our rule of life. As he says in the Book of Revelation, 'Behold, I stand at the door and knock. If anyone opens to me I will come unto him, and I will eat with him and he with me'. To accept Jesus' word is to accept Jesus himself; and we cannot have one without the other. We cannot profess faith in or admiration of Jesus and then show in our lives nothing of what he lays down for his followers — as, for example, in the Beatitudes, with their summons to poverty of spirit, to gentleness, mercy and peace-ableness in our relations with others, to purity of heart before God.

When, as here, Jesus speaks of our making our home in his word, the perspective, the emphasis is different, even if the content comes to the same thing. In this case it is Jesus who invites us to become his guest, to enter into and move freely and comfortably in his word as we move freely about and feel comfortable in our own home. It is through thinking about his word that we enter into the mind of Jesus, and into his heart. But, again, we can do so freely and comfortably only if the principles by which we live our lives and relate to others do not clash with, do not contradict the principles by which Jesus wishes his followers to live.

Jesus himself, in today's reading, tells us why it is important that we make our home in his word. 'What I speak of,' he says, 'is what I have seen with my Father'. That is to say, it is in living by the words of Jesus that we fulfil God's will for us in our lives. And again, as Jesus says here, it is by loving him that we show ourselves to be children of his Father and ours.

Fifth Week
Thursday
John 8:51-59

For several days now, our gospel readings have all concerned the question, Who is this Jesus? In various ways, Jesus has tried to convince his hearers of his unique sonship of God — and each approach he takes meets only with rejection. Finally, in today's reading, John brings this long-running confrontation to a dramatic end. Jesus takes to himself the divine name from the Old Testament: '. . . before ever Abraham came to be, I AM'; and his hearers take up stones to stone him to death for blasphemy.

We, of course, believe in the divinity of Jesus, believe him to be the Word made flesh, God become man. Why then, day by day in the Liturgy, this insistence on the divinity of our Lord? Perhaps the reason is this: next Sunday we begin to think about Jesus' last week of life, culminating in his passion and death. The sight of Jesus dead on the cross has its real impact only if we believe him to be God — for only that belief shows us the terrible reality of sin, and the wonder of the greater reality of God's merciful love for sinners.

Thus, seeing Jesus dead on the cross, we are moved to ask how it is that he, being the infinite Creator, should have willed to become man and, for my sins, to have come from eternal life to death in time. And seeing that the answer to that question is simply his love for us, we are then moved to ask ourselves, What have I done for Christ? What am I doing for Christ? What ought I to do for Christ?

It is knowing who he himself is and with this death in view that Jesus can say to us as he says to his hearers in today's reading: 'I tell you most solemnly, whoever keeps my word will never see death' — for his temporal death is our ransom from eternal death.

However, the saving power of his death becomes effective in us only if we 'keep his word'. Keeping his word means making his word the spirit in which we live our lives; it means making his word the motivating power of all we do.

When Jesus makes this promise, his hearers sieze on his words eagerly. Taking Jesus' words in a crassly physical sense, they see in them a sign of possession by the devil, evidence of madness, and the self-glorification of a braggart. But we, understanding their true meaning, seize on them even more eagerly, and with joy give thanks to the God who saves.

Fifth Week
Friday
John 10:31-42

The attempted stoning of Jesus with which today's reading begins is not the same incident with which yesterday's ended. That was during the feast recalling the Dedication of the Temple.

That circumstance and Jesus' words, 'The Father consecrated me and sent me into the world', provide yet another perspective on the continuing question, Who is this Jesus? By connecting the Feast of the Dedication of the Temple with his own being dedicated and sent into the world, Jesus is claiming to be the new, unique and definitive Temple.

The Temple of old was the place where God's glory dwelt: in Jesus, 'all the fulness of Godhead was pleased to dwell', and 'we have seen his glory — the glory that is his as the only-begotten Son of the Father'. The Temple was, also, the place of meeting between God and man: in Jesus, 'the Word was made flesh and dwelt among us', and in him God and man meet in a unique fashion, for Jesus is God become man. He shares our human life so that man can live henceforth with God's own life. Finally, the Temple was the one place in which sacrifice could be offered to God: Jesus, sacrificed on the cross, offers the one true sacrifice which fulfills and puts an end to all others.

On an earlier occasion, Jesus had already claimed to be the true and indestructible Temple of God's dwelling among men, when he said, after driving out the buyers and sellers, 'Destroy this temple (he was speaking of his own body) and in three days I shall raise it again'.

John begins his account of today's incident by noting that it was winter — a time of cold and darkness. But the real darkness was in the minds of Jesus' hearers, and the real cold was in their hearts. 'It was winter,' St Augustine comments, 'and they were cold, for they were unwilling to draw near to that divine fire. They were frozen for lack of love, yet they burned with the desire to do Jesus harm. They were there in his presence, yet they were far away; they pressed close to persecute him, but would not draw near by believing in him.'

Being physically near Jesus did most of his hearers no good. It is not our feet but our faith that brings us to him. We can draw close to him only through belief in him and love of him; but if we do come close to him then we will experience his love for us and experience, too, the Father's love which impelled him to love the world so much that he did not spare his own Son but delivered him us for us in order to make us temples of his own indwelling.

Fifth Week
Saturday
John 11:45-56

Today's reading tells us of the repercussions of Jesus' having raised Lazarus from the dead. In doing so, he had effectively issued his own death warrant. That raising of a dead man had caused many to accept Jesus as the long-awaited Messiah, the

Deliverer, in the sense in which they understood (or, rather, misunderstood) who the Messiah was and what his mission. The authorities fear an uprising of the people to install Jesus as Messiah; and that would mean a ruthless reaction by the Romans which would result in the destruction of the Temple and the nation. Jesus must die: there was nothing to fear from a dead Messiah, real or fraudulent.

The High Priest announces this: 'Better that one man should die for the people rather than the whole nation be destroyed'. John points out that his cynical, politically-motivated piece of opportunism was, ironically, prophetic and precise: 'He was prophesying that Jesus was going to die for the Jewish people, and not only for them, but also to bring together into one body all the scattered children of God'.

It is just as Jesus himself had said: 'I am the good Shepherd and I lay down my life for my sheep. And other sheep I have (the gentile nations) that are not of this sheepfold (the Jews). Them also I must bring.' But this bringing together of the whole human race — Jew and gentile, slave and free, male and female, so that all divisions between people are done away with and mankind becomes a new creation in Christ — all this can be done only through Jesus' conquest of the ultimate source of all division — that is to say, sin. And only Jesus can do this; for, as man, he can stand in the place of man the sinner, and, as God, in the place of the sinned against. Only he can be the point of reconciliation between God and man. Jesus freely accepts death, which is the great sign of sin in the world, and overcomes it in his resurrection. By his resurrection he shows that he has conquered sin itself and, thereby, the cause of all divisions among mankind as well as between mankind and God.

Truly it was necessary that one man should die rather than not merely one nation but the whole human race should not perish.

What Jesus did for the whole human race, he did also for each individual member of it — 'He loved *me*, and delivered himself up for *me*'. Astonished at this, rejoicing in this, I must ask myself, What ought I do to for him in return?

Holy Week

Passion (Palm Sunday)
Reading for the Procession of Palms:
Year A □ Matthew 21:1-11
Year B □ Mark 11:1-10 OR John 12:12-16
Year C □ Luke 19:28-40

Today is a day of triumph and of tragedy. Today, leaving the house of his friends at Bethany (Lazarus, Martha and Mary) Jesus begins a journey which will end only on Calvary. For this reason he will make of it an 'occasion' — not entering the Holy City on foot, as pilgrims customarily did, but riding.

It is difficult to avoid the conclusion that Jesus was deliberately giving a visual affirmation that it was he of whom Zechariah (in 9:9) spoke when he exhorted Jerusalem,

> Rejoice heart and soul, daughter of Zion!
> Shout with gladdness, daughter of Jerusalem!
> See now, your King comes to you;
> he is victorious, he is triumphant,
> humble, and riding on a donkey,
> on a colt, the foal of a donkey.

Luke makes quite a thing of Jesus' acquisition of the ass. He sends two of the disciples to a precise spot in a nearby village where they would find it. If they are challenged, they are to reply with grand simplicity, 'The Lord (that is, its real owner) has need of it'. One gets the impression that Luke means this incident to be taken as an example of Jesus' foreknowledge; but Jesus could, of course, have made a prior arrangement with its owner.

The young ass, it is insisted, had never been ridden. This was a necessary point, since animals set aside for sacred or royal use could not be put to other uses.

Jesus mounts the ass and moves onwards over the cloaks the people spread before him as custom then had it to soften the path of royalty. As he approaches Jerusalem, the throng sees the point of this symbolic action of his and cry out, 'Blessed is the king who comes in the name of the Lord'.

They are quoting Psalm 118(117):26 — a blessing on pilgrims to the Holy City which had come to be deemed messianic. Luke makes it clear that Jesus is the Messiah by replacing the 'he' of the original ('Blessed is he who comes') with the word 'King'; and he gives the crowd the words which he had given to the angels at the birth of Jesus.

And so we have the scene so vividly caught in Chesterton's poem, *The Donkey*:

The tattered outlaw of the earth
  Of ancient crooked will,
Starve, scourge, deride me: I am dumb,
  I keep my secret still.
Fools! For I also had my hour,
  One far fierce hour and sweet:
There was a shout about my ears.
  And palms before my feet ...

except that Luke does not mention palms as the other three gospels do. Luke does however mention that some Pharisees urged Jesus, 'Master, rebuke you followers' — a request not unknown to be made of Jesus by Christians in regard to other Christians. But Jesus roundly asserts that if the people fell silent the very stones would find a voice to acclaim him. It would be a shameful thing if our hearts were to prove harder than stones.

St Andrew of Crete well depicts what should be our part in today's proceedings:

Come, come, let us go together to the Mount of Olives. Together let us meet Christ who is returning today from Bethany and going of his own accord to that holy and blessed Passion to complete the mystery of our salvation.

Come, then, let us run with him as he presses on to his Passion. Let us imitate those who have gone out to meet him — not scattering olive branches or garments or palms in his path, but spreading ourselves before him as best we can with humility of soul and uprightness of purpose.

As Jesus' very presence impells the crowd to cast off their cloaks, so, through his Apostle he urges us to 'put off our old selves', as a cloak is discarded, in order to 'clothe ourselves in

Christ' and to 'wrap ourselves in humility to be servants of one another'.

So much for the triumph. But the day is also tragic — and Jesus has already wept over the city he is about to enter, lamenting its present blindness and future destruction. For the city would not recognise 'the day of its visitation'. For though the people had eyes to see what was being enacted before them, they did not have hearts to believe. And although the city was named for peace, it did not know 'the things that are to your peace'.

In his *Saint Luke*, G.B. Caird notes:

Luke began his Gospel by declaring that God had visited and redeemed his people (1:68) ... Now he tells us the day (of visitation) has come and Jerusalem is not ready for it. Yet the fact remains that God has visited his people either for salvation or for judgment; and, if Jerusalem will not have him as her Saviour, she must have him as her Judge.

We are, each of us, Jerusalem.

Holy Week
Monday
John 12:1-11

It is easy to visualise the scene put before us in today's reading, to appreciate the beauty of Mary's gesture and the eloquence of the silence in which it is performed. Just as the fragrance of Mary's ointment filled the whole house, so the memory of her deed fills the whole Church; and Jesus himself foretold (in Matthew's account of this incident) that, 'Wherever this gospel is preached, all over the world, what she has done will be told in memory of her'.

And yet her action is one which we, too, can perform. The early Fathers of the Church remind us that in serving the poor we anoint the feet of Christ. Jesus himself (in Mark's account) points out, 'You have the poor among you always so that you can do good to them when you will'. We must pray that we have that will always, and that love will always be the motive power of our doing good, as it was the well-spring of Mary's action here.

Jesus refers to the poor in answer to the hypocrisy of the disciples' response to Mary's action. Judas, himself a thief, asks, 'Why wasn't this perfume sold and the money given to the poor?' And the others join him in denouncing her. Mark says that they, in fact, 'rebuked her angrily'. The disciples' response is quite extraordinary: they were, after all, guests in the house and Mary was their hostess. She, together with her brother and sister, was a dearly loved friend of their Master, and he had only just recently raised the brother from the dead.

The disciples' bad manners, however, are nothing in comparison with their failure to see the real significance of Mary's action. Jesus points it out to them: 'She has anointed my body beforehand to prepare it for burial'; for, on Good Friday, the time will be too short for other than a hasty burial, and, on Easter morning, the humanity of Jesus will have already been anointed with the glory of the resurrection.

And so she has anointed the body beforehand to prepare it for burial. We who are the body of Christ must do likewise. By loving service of others we must prepare ourselves beforehand against the day of our own death and our meeting with Jesus who has told us, 'Whatever you did to the least of my brethren you did it to me. And whatever you did not do for them, you failed to do it to me'.

Holy Week
Tuesday
John 13:21-33, 36-38

'One of you will betray me,' says Jesus, referring to Judas; and, a little later, referring to Peter, 'Before cockcrow, you will have disowned me three times.'

Betrayal, or even a simple refusal of support, we find particularly hurtful; and Jesus was a man whose feelings were the same as ours. And yet, between these two predictions of betrayal and denial, Jesus rejoices and says, 'Now has the Son of Man been glorified; and, in him, God has been glorified'.

He rejoices because, with Judas' departing, the train of events has been set in motion which will end in his being 'lifted up' on the cross; and it was for this 'hour' of his being so lifted up that he, he said, had come into this world to give his life as a ransom for all.

Still, the impending betrayal weighs heavily on the heart of Jesus; and before he reveals his knowledge of it, the gospel tells us, 'he was profoundly disturbed in spirit'. Deeply distressed — it is an expression John also uses of the emotion which Jesus showed at the tomb of Lazarus. There Jesus confronted Satan in the form of death, 'the last enemy' as St Paul calls it. Here his emotion is the same, as he confronts his betrayal by Judas, into whose heart Satan has entered.

One of the Psalms says, 'Thus, even my friend whom I trusted, who ate my bread, has turned against me'. No one more than the Apostles had had such and so constant opportunity to learn the love, compassion, and gentleness of the heart of Jesus, or the power that was in him. And yet one of them betrayed him, another denied knowing him, and the rest, leaving him, fled.

Judas, then, had done more than share Jesus' table. From the start, he had been a chosen Apostle, sharing intimately the day-to-day life of Jesus, hearing him speak, watching him work miracles, seeing him at prayer and being himself taught by him to pray.

Peter, too, had experienced all this. More — he had, when Jesus asked, 'Who do you say I am?', answered, 'You are the Christ, the Son of the living God' — a confession he will deny when three times he will say, 'I do not know the man'.

In the gospel references to the betrayal of Jesus, the emphasis on 'one of the Twelve' suggests that neither Jesus nor the Gospel-writers could get over the fact that betrayal came from among the closest associates of Jesus. And we, all of us, who have been baptised are associates of Jesus.

Holy Week
Wednesday
Matthew 26:14-25

Today's gospel takes up where Monday's left off after Mary's anointing the feet of Jesus. As yesterday, the theme is Judas' betrayal of Jesus; and, again, the writer's emphasis is on the fact that the betrayer was one of the Twelve.

Judas' motive in deciding on betrayal is utterly baffling. Was it that, being the only Judean among the Twelve, he felt an outsider? Was he repelled by the course Jesus was taking, and rejected it? Or did he think to compel Jesus to take another course? Was he trying to salvage something for himself out of the inevitable wrack of Jesus' 'career'? We simply do not know.

The gospel writer directs us to the prophecy of Zechariah: 'That day, the dealers who were watching me realised that this had been a word from the Lord. I then said to them, 'If you think it right, give me my wages ...'. And they weighed out my wages — thirty shekels of silver. But the Lord told me, 'Throw it into the treasury — this princely sum at which they have valued me!' (11:11-13).

This, then, is perhaps the terrible truth which Judas' actions demonstrate — that it is possible to hold God cheap; and we do so in some degree when we prefer anything to God, neglect to pray or to attend to his presence in our lives, or care little for his will for us. It is not that we, as it were, consciously weigh God in a scales against something else and find that something preferable. We would not be so silly. It is just that sometimes we act as if we did.

The thirty shekels of silver have another meaning. In the Law of Moses, thirty such shekels was the value placed on the life of a slave. It reminds us of St Paul's words concerning Jesus: 'His nature was, from the first, divine. But he emptied himself, taking the condition of a slave ... and accepting death on a cross'. Paul prefaces these words with, 'In your minds you must be the same as Christ Jesus'. This, then, is the worth at which we should value ourselves. We are like Jesus to the extent that (as he himself says) we make ourselves least of all and servant of all — just as he himself says that he came into the world not to be served but to serve, and to give his life for all.